# THE ROAD TO DENTAL SCHOOL

## A Pre-Dental Guide

## CORY TSUHAKO

# The Road to Dental School

*A Pre-Dental Guide for Dental School*

Cory M. Tsuhako

Published by Cory Tsuhako Enterprises.

Books by Cory Tsuhako:

The Birth of a Business

Fatherlessness

All pictures are from Google's free images.

# Table of Contents

# ACKNOWLEDGEMENTS

No one applies to dental school without the help of supportive people. I would like to thank my mother who inspired me to go into healthcare and to my uncle who inspired me to go into the dental profession. My grandparents were my biggest supporters and I would like to thank them on these pages.

I would also like to thank the wonderful dentists who helped me along the way when I was a pre-dental student and, later, when I owned a dental laboratory. Your generosity was appreciated!

I would like to thank Curt Hardaway for his wonderful proofreading and editing skills. He is the best!

Lastly I would like to thank my pre- and post-dental advisors who encouraged me to consider looking into business as a major when I was stuck                              on                              dental.

# Preface

**WELCOME TO** *The Road to Dental School.* It has taken many years to process this information and to present it to you, the pre-dental student. It is written for high school and college students wanting to know more about the pre-dental process, for parents wanting to learn about the major, and for people wondering if they should go back to school to change their careers. It was my goal to portray a realistic picture into the life of a pre-dental student.

## MY STORY

Beverly Hills, Rodeo Drive

**MY PRE-DENTAL JOURNEY** began on a glorious Southern California day. I was working in Beverly Hills as a dental technician after having recently returned from a vacation in Maui. I was rested and ready for a new challenge, or at least that's what I thought. I was walking among the gleaming luxury cars when an idea hit me that would change my life forever—I decided to become a dentist.

## PARENTS

# COOPERATION

**IF YOU ARE THE PARENT** of a future dentist this may be a helpful book for you. It is written to give you a look into the process of applying to dental school and what you can expect from it. This is an incredibly difficult goal—similar to medical school. If you are a parent of a future dentist expect to sacrifice in terms of money and emotions, and it's never too early to start a college savings account.

Parental support is important during this time. While the rewards are great, failure is a possibility and threatens the student at every exam. Roughly nine out of ten don't make it and the student is often left demoralized without any idea what to do next.

**W**ELCOME to my therapy session. As I started to write this book, I realized it was going to be cheaper than therapy, plus there's the benefit of leaving something behind after death. I want to thank you for meeting me on the pages like this. I hope that you find it informational, interesting, and above all entertaining.

*"I came from an impoverished background, the child of a divorce, and wanted to become a dentist."*

If you are a student considering dental school I'd like to take you on a trip. I've opened the pages of my *ten years* as a pre-dental student to help you to make an informed decision on whether to choose this career. Please be warned, if you are easily discouraged then you should stop reading now.

Many years ago, this was my reality. I had taken the courses, applied to dental school and when I got there the doors were closed.

## So you want to become a dentist?

The best place to begin is from the beginning. That's the decision to become a dentist. You should give yourself plenty of time to make this important decision and not rush it. It's probably a good idea to test, confirm, and re-test your performances as you go along before announcing your plans to your family and friends. This is a long, hard road and you should give yourself permission to change your mind a few times and to compare dentistry with other professions.

When is the best time to decide to become a dentist? Some know when they are in high school; others may find the calling when they are in college. And still others may change their careers to give dentistry a try. Just like we are born into this world, a pre-dental student usually arrives into the profession. But once you start this goal, there will be no turning back. The lure of the good life will cast a cloud over your future endeavors and will follow you in everything that you do. This is not an easy road.

# RESEARCH

**WHAT KIND OF** people become dentists? As a group they are highly intelligent, good with their hands, have a burning desire to help their communities, thrive on a challenge, and are usually warm and friendly people. Dentistry offers them an opportunity to earn a good living, to own their own business (although that is changing) and to serve their communities.

Be sure to assess your performance. You don't want to be competing on your weakness—I mean if math and science is not your strength then being in classes with pre-meds is not going to help. The courses are graded on the curve and I've seen classmates unsuccessfully try over and over to pass a class.

# COMMITMENT

**BE PREPARED TO** give this goal all you have, but know there is a possibility that you may fail. If you come from a disadvantaged background the chance of failure increases. Some students suffer from what is known as "barriers to achievement."

When I decided that I wanted to become a dentist, I didn't access my skills. In fact I didn't meet with a pre-dental advisor at the community college that I attended. I wanted to complete my math classes before meeting with someone who might try to talk me out of it.

# THE PRE-DENTAL LIFE

**WELCOME TO THE FASCINATING** world of the pre-dental student. Your time will be spent learning the discoveries of the world's greatest scientists such as Einstein, Darwin, and Pauling, and by the time you finish you'll be using their formulas at will. In time you will grow accustomed to the smell of formaldehyde, you will fearlessly light a Bunsen burner, and (if successful) you will one day provide a great service to the wealthy, famous and poor. The day you become a dentist will be a day that will change your life, but while you study you will have to battle burnout, fatigue, and your competition.

The life of a pre-dental student is filled with long days, sleepless nights and incredible stress. Your emotions will often be accompanied by feelings of impending doom, with potential failure lurking around every corner, every exam, yet you must maintain a cheerful personality for advisors. It's a goal that asks a lot of a person, yet promises incredible rewards to the victor.

# DENTISTRY TODAY

**THERE HAS NEVER** been a better time to become a dentist. The job of a dentist was ranked number one in healthcare by the U.S. News & World Report with an average yearly wage of $166,810 by the Bureau of Labor Statistics. If you add the respect, status, doctor's lifestyle, and wealth it creates, it's a hard profession to beat, but the dental industry is changing. Technology is giving dentists options that didn't exist decades ago, but these systems are expensive and become obsolete in a few years. One of the benefits of the CAD/CAM is that a crown can be made in under two hours.

Dental trends:

-

- General dental services are declining

- Specialty services are increasing

- Insurance companies are lowering their reimbursements

- Difficulty in raising prices

- The barriers of entry are increasing

- Digital impressions

- More females are graduating dental school

Large corporate finance companies are managing professionally run dental groups. The result is less solo practices, more competition, and higher costs needed to open a dental office. While venture capitalists are entering the industry, the need for dentists will always remain since they cannot "drill and fill," but they can bill.

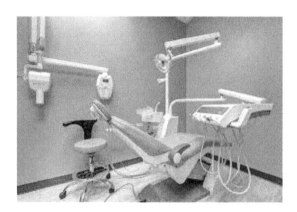

The dental practice is undergoing a technological revolution. From the CAD/CAM to social media, future dental students are fortunate to be exposed to the new technologies while in school. A few years ago people wouldn't believe that computers would be making crowns. One thing for certain is the dental and healthcare systems are changing and these changes are making it harder for the solo practitioner. The successful dentist must manage their careers and practices amidst changing healthcare policies and a corporate                                                                    culture.

# CHAPTER TWO

# Your School

University of Texas, San Antonio

**WHERE YOU TAKE YOUR SCIENCE CLASSES** is crucial to your success. On the West Coast there are schools that are known for weeding out their pre-professional students while others are known for providing pre-science classes to working adults and for their generous grading.

## Avoid getting B's and C's

Once you declare yourself a pre-dental student, your job is to get A's in the sciences. This is no easy feat and is a worthy accomplishment. What makes it so hard? All your classmates want A's and a lot of them are pre-medical students. So all things being equal you should take your prerequisites where you have the best chance to get good grades. If I was to do it over again, I would research several schools before taking general chemistry, biology, physics and organic chemistry. I would also consider taking some classes at a community college at night.

## Why do you want to become a dentist?

During your pre-dental years someone will ask you, "Why do you want to become a dentist?" This is similar to your sales pitch. It becomes an important question to answer since it's on the essay part of the application. It also says a lot about you as an applicant and what motivates you.

To most students this is probably going to be much harder than you think. Make friends with the library staff because you will be spending a lot of time there. But you will not be alone; your classmates will be there too.

University of Maryland

## HISTORY

**THE FIRST DENTAL SCHOOL IN AMERICA** was the Baltimore College of Dental Surgery in 1828. It was renamed the University of Maryland School of Dentistry. Today there are over sixty dental schools that produce over 5,000 new dentists every year.

# HIGH SCHOOL

**YOU HAVE A GREAT OPPORTUNITY** if you start from high school. You'll have more time to get to know your dentist and to build on your math and science skills. You can join clubs, participate in sports, network with alumni, attend concerts and museums, volunteer, and will have the benefit of having more time to progress in your dental career.

You should know that pre-dental classes move quickly. You need the studying techniques to master new material in an efficient manner. Some of my classmates were high school honor students and they complained about how different college was from high school. Assume that the classes will be much harder, with a deeper level of understanding—this way you won't be surprised. I took a regular biology course in a community college and when I took pre-dental biology I was shocked how fast the chapters flew by.

Getting an early start can place you in general chemistry rather than intro to chemistry. Most schools require new students to take a chemistry placement exam.

Dental school is an investment of eight years or more. Four years of pre-dental followed by four years of dental school. At best you will be 26 years old when you graduate. Many will be older by the time they pass the boards. Your education is going to take awhile so have fun when you can.

Dental school prerequisites:

- General chemistry: 8 units

- Organic chemistry: 8 units

- Biology: 8 units

- Physics: 8 units

- English: 8 units

- Math: basic, pre-algebra, algebra, geometry, trigonometry, calculus.

Get familiar with the dental school's websites where you'll find information regarding pre-admissions workshops, admission facts, timelines, financial aid information and admission requirements. Why? Some schools may differ and require additional prerequisites. For example one school may require biochemistry while another may request cell biology. There is also valuable information on what you can expect in dental school. I would get familiar with the websites of the schools that I am planning to apply to.

Looking back, I would have done a test to see if I really enjoyed chemistry, rather than announcing to family, friends, and co-workers that I wanted to be a dentist. This would have made it easier to change my path later down the road. It can be embarrassing when people ask how it went or what you've been up to.

One of my co-workers told people he wanted to be a brain surgeon while he was still in high school. A better answer might have been to say, "I'm looking into the medical industry." Don't be in a rush to tell everyone that you are considering being a dentist. Sometimes it's better to keep your plans a secret and to enjoy life and to find some things you are good at. For example, if you can excel in a sport, play a musical instrument or be a leader in something, it can help. Dental schools are looking for leaders.

## Build on your learning skills

The typical pre-dental science course has two classes—a lecture and a lab. In your lab you'll have to prepare lab reports on your findings and this scientific writing is different from other subjects. The lab reports often include a description of the experiment, the performance of an experiment, collecting data, and interpretation of the findings. You can possibly include a diagram, or maybe a graph, and it usually ends with a conclusion of your findings.

# BIOLOGY LAB

A high school biology lab

BIOLOGY IS THE OBSERVATION of life, from looking at slides under a microscope, to conducting experiments on plants, to performing dissections; you will be developing your powers of observation. Think of a room of dead animals in jars and the smell of formaldehyde.

*Pre-dental tips:* be prepared for the lab practical exam where you will walk around the room, look into a microscope and name the slide or specimen.

Oscillatoria can be dyed purple, green, and blue—don't let this surprise you. When you look through the microscope and think that it's a green organism, well it can be dyed pink. Don't let them catch you on this one.

# CHEMISTRY LAB

High school chemistry lab

IMAGINE WALKING INTO a laboratory to an intimidating set-up of beakers, hoses, and fire. Then you are given a jar of powder and realize you are going to have to assemble the same thing and perform an experiment on it where you will record data, then prepare a report. Usually they give you a few days or a week, but they might spring a surprise and ask for it in class.

*Pre-dental tips:* precipitate is something turning into a solid. For example if you pour a liquid in a solution and it starts to clump, then that's a precipitate.

There is no horse play in a chemistry lab as it can be dangerous with the fire and combustible chemicals.

Always read the lab experiments before coming to class.

The ability to wash dishes and to keep a clean sink will be an unexpected benefit of your education. If things don't work out in dentistry there is always the option to work as a dishwasher.

# PHYSICS LAB

High school physics lab

**IN PHYSICS LAB** you'll work in groups and will put together an electrical power system to conduct experiments where you will perform, record, and analyze data. I'd encourage you to watch some YouTube videos to get a glimpse of what kind of experiments you will be doing. The best advice I can give you is to read the textbook and the lab procedures manual before going to class.

Remember to get along with your classmates, the lab assistants, teachers, administration, and the all-important advisors. It's not all studying once you get into your university. You are now part of the university family and hopefully will become a valuable alumni member. Your college experience can be dynamic, challenging and fun!

# The Older Student

**I BEGAN** the pre-dental process in my early twenties, but by the time I applied to dental school I was an "older student." Within the boundaries of the university system there are non-traditional older students who drop back into school to change careers, learn new skills, or to finish their degrees—some of them are pre-dental students. Is there an age limit to applying to dental school? Students over 40 are rarely accepted into dental school.

"Hello sir," the bookstore clerk asked me. I could tell she thought I was an instructor . . . Oh the memories of being among the youngsters—and being one of the oldest in the class. How I miss those days. Hopefully your maturity and life experiences will help you to deal with the different ages and personalities you will be faced with while you develop relationships with your young classmates.

Your family and friends might not understand when you tell them that you don't have time to "hang out" like before. Between studying, preparing for exams, and doing your lab reports you will be busy. If you are not working consider yourself blessed. If you are working you will be at a disadvantage and will have to manage your time carefully. Hopefully you will be able to enjoy your college experience—being active in science clubs, special research opportunities, building friendships, volunteering, and attending cultural events.

While you are under the stress of taking your pre-dental classes, a hobby or outlet can help relieve that stress and gain perspective. Spending time with family and friends, a walk in the park, taking in a baseball game—sometimes you need a break from the pre-dental activities.

One of the things that bothered me the most were my family and friends moving on with their lives. My pool of friends slowly shrank as they got married, bought homes, and raised their families. The worst was the weddings. I finally had to stop torturing myself and quit going—losing some of my closest friends in the process.

Studying with other older students helps as you will have things in common, but don't get too attached—many will fall away and go back to their jobs, or will change to an easier goal. During this time your classmates can be crucial for your success, so it's important to give them their proper respect since you need their support.

Study hard, even though there is a chance you may not make it. You certainly want to access your chances wisely. It helps to have some Plan B ideas while you are pursuing this goal. If you're not careful the years can start to add up.

# WORKING ADULTS

If you have to work you might want to let your employer know of your plans. There may be times that you may need to take time off to prepare for exams. Having an employer who encourages you can be very important during this time.

Winning support from those you live with is critical. If you don't your life will be a mess. This will be an adjustment phase as you'll have less time and less money. Your family can be a strength or it can give you stress of ruined relationships.

During my time as a pre-dent I saw many adults "drop back" into school to change their careers. Some of these included:

A computer programmer who went back to school to become an optometrist.

An accountant going back to school to become a dentist.

A business executive who went back to school to become a dentist.

A dental hygienist who continued going to school to become a dentist.

An engineer who went back to school to become a dentist.

A military veteran going to school to become a medical doctor, then changing his goal to become a biology teacher.

A high school biology teacher who wanted to be a dentist, then went back to teaching.

A nurse who was pre-med and went on to a master's degree in nursing.

What was the secret? I noticed that students who had a history of success had a much higher acceptance rate. They had earned their degrees, excelled in their careers and now were trying to get into professional school. A large percentage of these older adults came from supportive families and were generally confident about their futures.

On the other hand I saw many minority classmates drop out. The school I attended is from an urban section of Los Angeles and is attended by students that make up the "barriers to achievement" group. They worked a lot of hours and were not as confident as they struggled financially and scholastically.

# Degrees

**DURING** my time as a pre-dental student I noticed that students who had already earned their degrees seemed to have an advantage over the ones who hadn't. They also had more confidence and work experience. They had money saved for their education so they didn't have to work and had their support system in place. Most of these students accomplished their goals and are now working as health professionals.

# Your Major

**ANY MAJOR** is fine as long as the required pre-dental classes are met. I have seen science, business, and music majors get into dental school. Having a non-science major may result in a higher GPA, but taking additional science classes may give you an advantage once you get in. These are some of the science classes that you may see in dental school:

- Anatomy
- Biochemistry
- Histology
- Pathology
- Pharmacology
- Physiology

Taking dental lab classes could be helpful and may result in a higher GPA, but the number of community colleges offering them is declining.

# Your Professors

*I'LL NEVER FORGET my first day in chemistry class. I had to take basic math all the way to calculus—a result of my public school education and being a music major. While I listened to the chemistry professor I realized this was going to be harder than I thought.*

Some of your professors wanted to be medical doctors, but they didn't make it. Now they are responsible for educating tomorrow's doctors. They are doctors, not as MDs or dentists but as PhDs. Some of them are tough on future medical doctors. Their preferred students are those specializing in chemistry, biology or physics.

It pays to get on their good side, if you can find it. How do you do this? By asking them questions in their office. It may be uncomfortable, but you are going to have to spend time with them.

Don't expect your professors to care about your future. They see many students fall to the wayside during the pre-med/pre-dental process. Your plight is not new to them. They are remarkable people, but they can be damaging to your goal. At this stage you may consider quitting, a lot of people do. I'll never forget my chemistry instructor standing before us on the first day, *"I hold all the points, you have to take them from me . . . and I don't want to give them to you."*

## Who has your A's?

It pays to ask around to find out who the "easier" teachers are. A reputation usually follows a teacher. Some are known to be generous graders while others are known to be demanding as if their purpose on earth is to weed out hopeful doctors. Your job will be to avoid these types . . . or at least to survive them.

# THE OFFICE VISIT

Your instructors are busy people and they know the game. You want a positive letter of recommendation. Keep your visits brief and respect their time. You definitely don't want to wear out your welcome.

You might prepare questions in advance for your office visits so you don't waste your opportunity. In time some of your professors will be among your most trusted and admired mentors while others may earn your disdain.

The first time I went to a professor's office was a requirement. I timidly knocked on the thick office door hoping he wouldn't be there.

Knock, knock.

The door opened.

"Come in," he said smiling. I noticed that he looked more human up close.

"Have a seat," the old grumpy professor told me. He motioned for me to sit in a chair next to him.

"Why don't you do one of the problems that we went over in lecture today?"

I took a seat in his small office and struggled to do the problem. Either you have read the chapters before the lecture and can ask intelligent questions or you are like me, lost during the lecture and are looking for a way out, but he leaves you to struggle longer than is comfortable. You start to squirm. Just a heads-up that this is a test, an opportunity, and a bonding moment all at once. He is getting to know you and seeing if you need help, and how prepared you are. It may happen to you and you should be ready. Are you up to date on the lectures? You should be.

## THE WEEDING OUT PROCESS

Will you be weeded out? Hopefully not, but I must confess . . . some of my smartest classmates were weeded out during this process. What happened?

- Unable to deal with the stress of the classes
- Anxiety attacks
- Lack of confidence

They decided this goal was too risky and made alternative plans regarding their future.

Not everyone who wants to be a doctor will become one. Our healthcare system is not built that way. So there must be a thinning out of applicants. During these times, it sure helps to have a supportive ear. You and your classmates are in a "group suffering" situation. They are your competition, yet you need their support. Your professors are important, but there is someone even more important.

# Your Advisor

**YOUR ADVISOR** is there to give you guidance, support, and honesty during this time and is your most valuable person in this process. When times get rough and you need an honest opinion, your advisor will be the one whose judgment you can depend on. It was my advisor who recommended that I change my major and to complete my degree.

Sometimes your advisor is also your professor. It's always a good decision to take your classes with your advisors as they usually appreciate the support and can judge your abilities in class. You need to develop this relationship and enrolling in their classes is one way to do it.

Remember that your advisor may be asked to submit an evaluation of your leadership abilities, cooperativeness, dependability, ability to accept suggestions, creativeness, and friendliness with classmates, advisors, and professors, as well as other characteristics. It's in your best interests to be on good terms with all the teachers on the pre-dental committee (if there is one) and science instructors, since they hold your future in their hands.

In most cases you will be assigned an advisor who you don't know and who doesn't know you. Keep this in mind when advisors are recommending classes for you. They don't know your situation at home or work, or your family responsibilities. You have to be in charge of your future and cannot blindly accept their advice.

*I had transferred to a new school and I met with a pre-dental advisor. He gave me a schedule with chemistry, physics, and music theory. He didn't take into consideration that I worked full-time and hadn't taken geometry yet.*

## Advisors can't read your mind

When should you find an advisor? The earlier the better. Probably high school is the best time to have a quality pre-dental advisor. It takes planning to manage a successful career in healthcare. One never knows where they may end in this dynamic and changing landscape.

# Old Exams

**ONE REASON TO** network with your classmates is to get your instructors' old exams. At times this can be a wonderful study aid. So how do you get into this select group? You have to network with your senior classmates, well-connected classmates, or people who have already taken the classes.

Is this legal? I'm not sure and you will have to learn the policies of your school. I know that some students don't rely on old exams. I heard of someone who relied on them so much she had to retake all her science classes again.

In dental school and in life a large percentage of your success will depend on how well you get along with people and who you know. Is using their old exams ethical? Maybe, maybe not. It depends on whether your classmates have them as well. I don't support the practice, but it does exist both before and during dental school. The key is to not need them, but to know where they are in case you do.

*Pre-dental tip:* this is done entirely in secret. If a professor finds out that you have their old exams you might be expelled so please know the rules and regulations of your school.

# Your Classmates

**EVERY CLASS HAS** its cast of characters. Who makes up your class? Potential medical doctors, dentists, professors, optometrists, and chiropractors, among others. Enjoy the intellectual diversity while it lasts. There are few opportunities in life that brings together a special mix of people like this.

*Your best friend:* maybe you share the same goal, major, age, or nationality, but you'll know them as the person you can trust.

*Your good friends:* you've been in the same classes for a semester or two and know that you can rely on them for support, lecture notes and studying together.

*The pin-up:* the one girl or guy who everyone wants to date yet avoids—tread carefully as studying with them can be very distracting.

*The middle child:* this person wants to study with everyone in the class.

*The wheeler dealer:* this is the person with old exams from the last three years. Of course you have to give them something in return—like another test to add to their collection.

*The pre-meds:* they like to pick on the pre-dents like their younger siblings.

*The superhero pre-med*: this is the person trying to do everything at once.

*The future professors*: these students are in school to learn to teach in high school or to become university professors. Your professors love these folks.

*The pre-dents:* it makes sense to get to know them as they are both your support and competition.

*The rivals:* these are almost everyone as you are graded on a curve. One day you may be best friends, the next day strangers.

*The dark cloud:* there may be that one person who looks like they can't handle the pressure and sometimes they have a massive breakdown.

# YOUR SCIENCE GPA

Does your science GPA include math? Yes!

Does it include that astronomy class that you took as a general elective? Yes!!

Does it include dental assisting classes taken at a community college? Yes!!!

## Don't experiment with your science GPA!

These classes are included in the science GPA:

- 
    Science classes
-

- Math classes

- Computer classes (some)

- Dental assisting

- Dental hygiene

- Dental laboratory technology

- Dental classes

- Medical classes

You will be busy with opportunities from clubs, volunteering, studying for classes, shadowing dentists, working, all while taking important classes. It's a balancing act, but your grades remain as permanent reminders of how well you can manage your time and your life.

# CHAPTER THREE

## The Big Three

**THE DAY YOU** become a "pre-dental" student your big three classes will be biology, chemistry, and physics. Do well in these classes and you will earn the respect of classmates, professors, relatives and the all-important advisor. All pre-professional students know this, yet not all of them are able to earn A's in these classes. Biology will test your memory; chemistry will test your science knowledge and math, while physics will challenge your science and trigonometry skills. These three classes are a good indicator whether you will get into dental school. The most important of these classes is organic chemistry.

A DAY IN THE LIFE OF A PRE-DENTAL STUDENT

*Today is my first day at my new school, Cal State University, Dominguez Hills. I transferred from El Camino (a community college) and my first semester is chemistry, physics and music theory. I changed my hours at work from 9-5 to 5-midnight.*

*Chemistry seems harder than I expected. After taking the placement exam they put me in introduction to chemistry, not chemistry 1A. I'm not surprised as this is the first chemistry class in my life. I never had a 5-unit class. Classes are mornings Mondays, Wednesdays and Fridays with a three hour lab during the week. My physics class is Tuesday and Thursdays with a three hour lab 1-4 pm on Thursdays. Then there is music theory on Tuesdays and Thursday nights. I'm worried that I should have taken geometry before trigonometry. I'll have to take geometry during summer school at a community college.*

*Things are crazy busy, from attending lectures, going to lab, doing homework, preparing lab reports, studying for exams and keeping up with the reading.*

## Take time to master the material

If I could do it again I would take my time, enjoy the process and master the science material. Many of my classmates took heavy loads of classes while they kept up an active social and community life. Some of them dropped out quickly. It makes sense to learn the material the first time. You will see it again on the DAT (Dental Admission Test).

# Biology

**FOR THOSE STUDENTS** who haven't taken pre-dental biology, it requires a lot of memorization. The year-long course will take you on a journey from the atom to the primates.

**Key concepts:**

- **Cell structure**
- **Life and evolution**
- **Genetics**
- **The Kingdoms**
- **Human anatomy and physiology**
- **Reproduction**

**Darwin's theory of evolution** - states that all living things came from one common ancestor and those living things use energy to grow, reproduce, show hereditary variations, adapt and respond.

**Kingdoms** - Monera, Protista, Fungi, Plantae, and Animalia.

**Genetics** - Mendel; the Punnett square; how genes act; how DNA replicates; translation of DNA/RNA and cracking the genetic code.

**Molecules:** the four major types are - carbohydrates, lipids, proteins and nucleic acids.

**Cells** - are the unit of structure, function and heredity.

**Cell biologist** - some of the tools of the cell biologist include the ultracentrifuge, the compound microscope, the phase contrast microscope and the electron microscope.

**Cell theory** - cells are the functional units of life and everything is composed of cells. All cells are preexisting and may behave in groups.

**Cytoplasm** - is the semifluid substance inside the cell.

**Nucleus** - the main part of the cell. It contains the chromosomes of DNA. It directs reproduction, metabolism and growth.

**Mitochondrion** - ATP energy is stored here; it has its own DNA and is a power generator of the cell.

**DNA** - is the blueprint (contains genes) for the proteins produced in a cell. It cannot produce uracil, but manufactures three different kinds of RNA in the nucleus; all are involved in protein formation.

**DNA** - has coded information, can self-replicate and is mutable.

**DNA** and **RNA** - are involved in the genetic code.

**Nucleic acids** - chains of nucleotides which are the units that combine to form DNA and RNA.

**Autotrophs** - can produce their own food through photosynthesis.

**Heterotrophs** - cannot produce their own energy source.

**Photosynthesis** - light energy, or the process of making food from carbon dioxide and water by the use of chlorophyll and sunlight. The role of light is to split the H2O molecule.

**Chloroplasts** - are found only in plant cells and are a storage bin of color.

**Ecology** - the study of organisms and their environments.

**Energy** - is made by the chemical reactions that occur in a cell. There are a variety of chemical forces from mechanical, heat, electrical, light and radiation.

**Energy** - comes in two forms: potential and kinetic.

**First law of thermodynamics** - energy balances out.

**Second law of entropy** - says that energy that transforms is never 100% efficient.

**Anaerobic** - able to survive in the absence of free oxygen.

**Aerobic** - capable of living in the presence of oxygen.

**Carnivore** - a meat eater.

**Herbivore** - a plant eater.

**Omnivore** - eats both plants and meat.

**Human anatomy and physiology** - circulatory systems and the regulation of blood flow.

**Immune system** - white blood cells, antibodies.

**Respiration** – lungs, blood and gases.

**Digestion and nutrition** - oral cavity, salivary gland, pharynx, epiglottis, larynx, esophagus, stomach, intestines, and the liver, bile duct, gall bladder, appendix, stomach, pylorus, pancreas, small and large intestine.

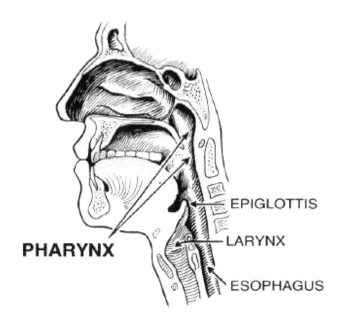

EPIGLOTTIS

PHARYNX

LARYNX

ESOPHAGUS

**Carbohydrates** - complex sugars which are large groups of organic molecules; monosaccharides (one); disaccharides (double); and polysaccharides (many).

**Sugars** - galactose (milk); sucrose (table sugar); glucose (blood); fructose (fruit); maltose (malt) and lactose (milk sugar).

**Skeletons and muscles** - smooth and cardiac muscles.

**Bone marrow** - is the site of the formation of blood cells.

**Muscular system** - smooth, skeletal, cardiac.

**Skeletal muscle** - actin is thin while myosin is thick.

**Endocrine glands** - glands that an animal manufactures as hormones and secretes them into the bloodstream. Examples include pituitary, adrenal, thyroid, parathyroid, the ovary and testis, the placenta and part of the pancreas.

**Pituitary gland** - posterior and anterior.

**Posterior pituitary** - oxytoxin and vasopressin.

**Anterior pituitary** - growth hormones, prolactin, thyrotropic hormone, adrenocorticotropic hormone, follicle-stimulating hormone and the luteinizing hormone.

### Pituitary and Pineal Glands

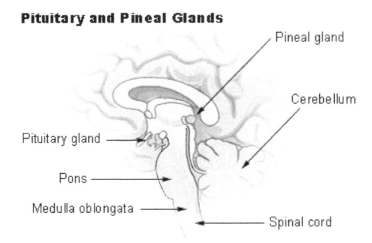

**Hormones** - chemical messengers that target specific cells and tissue.

**Brain** - is made up of neurons and performs basic to complex functions from breathing to releasing hormones.

**Cortex** - the grey matter of the brain, the outer layer of the cerebrum.

**Medulla** - the most important part of the brain.

**Reproduction** - mitosis and meiosis.

**Adrenal medulla** - associated with epinephrine which increases blood pressure and heart rate.

*DAT tips:* Common concepts that occur on the DAT.

**Hardy-Weinberg** - genotype frequencies in a population will remain constant from generation to generation in the absence of other influences.

**Cell biology** - study of cell structure and function.

**Vocabulary** - centriole, chromosomes, cytoplasm, endoplasmic reticulum, golgi apparatus, lysosome, mitochondria, nucleolus, nucleus, nuclear membrane, plasma membrane, ribosome, vacuole.

**Centriole** - the sites for microtubules spindles that are used in cell division.

**Chromosomes** - the site of the genetic information in most organisms.

**Cytoplasm** - the living matter inside the cell, not including the nucleus.

**Endoplasmic reticulum** - where the synthesis of proteins occurs.

**Golgi apparatus** - stores proteins for secretion.

**Lysosomes** - digests macromolecules.

**Mitochondria** - known as the powerhouse of the cell—it produces 95% of all ATP in the cell.

**Nucleolus** - produces the rRNA for ribosomes.

**Nucleus** - contains DNA and is the control center of the cell.

**Plasma membrane** - the thin bilayer made up of lipids and proteins.

**Ribosome** - site of protein synthesis.

**Vacuole** - a space within the cytoplasm of a cell that is filled with liquid, air or water.

**Specialized Eukaryotic Cells and Tissues**

The nervous system:

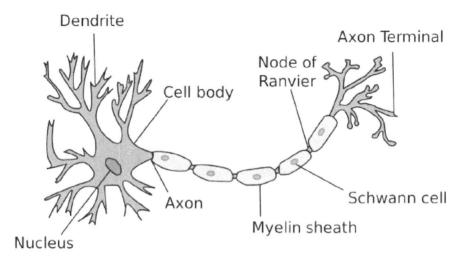

**Axon** - the long threadlike part of a nerve cell that carries the nerve impulse.

**Dentrites** - form the connections with the axons of neurons and transmits the nerve impulses.

**Myelin sheath** - insulates the axons of neurons that allow a faster transmission of nerve impulses.

**Nodes of Ranvier** - non-myelinated sections of a nerve cell axon.

**Sympathetic and parasympathetic** - both make up the two divisions of the autonomic nervous system.

**Sympathetic nervous systems** - increased breathing and heart rate and dilation of pupils.

**Parasympathetic nervous systems** - activities that occur when the body is at rest. An example is a slower heart rate.

**Operon** - a unit of genomic DNA.

**Pulmonary** - lungs and the heart.

**Biological systems** - complex network of organisms.

**Viruses** - can be crystallized and can last years. A virus needs a host and reproduces by invading a host cell. In the lysogenic phase DNA is inserted in the host chromosome, while the lytic phase destroys the host cell.

There are three ways a substance can pass through a **plasma membrane** - through pores, dissolving, or binding to a carrier. It is made up of proteins and phospholipids.

The **three germ layers** - ectoderm, mesoderm, endoderm.

**Circulation** - arteries, capillaries, veins.

**Arteries** - thick-walled and carry blood away from the heart under high pressure.

**Capillaries** - very thin narrow vessels, cover a large surface area. The exchange of gases and materials occurs here.

**Veins** - receives blood from the capillaries and returns it to the heart.

The **heart** is four chambered:

Right atrium

Right ventricle

Left atrium

Left ventricle

"Atrium" in Latin means "waiting room." The atrium is a holding area.

**An example of a DAT Problem**

This animal eats plants only.

a)
    Carnivore
b)
    Omnivore
c)
    Herbivore
d)

All of the above

e)

None of the above

**Solution**

Answer is C.

Your science classes are relative to you earning a high score. Enjoy the learning as you will come upon it again for your DAT.

# General Chemistry

**THE MORE** you work with the problems the more you will retain. Chemistry is like learning an instrument; it helps to have people to work out with. Finding a study partner can help in the learning process the same way that musicians "jam" together.

One bit of advice that I would like to give you is to be friendly (first impressions *do* last) on the first day of class. Sit where you feel like you will get to know your classmates. It might be a good idea to go early on your first day of class. Why? Some of these classmates might save you in the event that you should miss a class. This goal is going to require sacrifice and long hours studying and making friends along the way helps to improve the experience.

- First impressions are important
- Don't miss a class!
- Don't miss a lab!

There may come a time when you feel that you need a day off. This isn't a good idea. It makes it look like you don't care. In some classes you might have to retake the lab on a make-up day or you may even be dropped. In some schools, once you are dropped . . . you can never return.

**Atom**

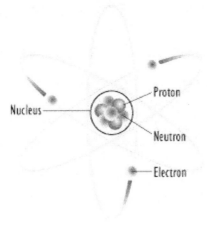

- Structure: protons, neutrons, and electrons

- The nucleus is central and highly concentrated

- Sometimes the mass number is referred to as atomic mass

**Electrons** - are moving fast. The farther away the electrons are from the nucleus, the more potential energy they possess. Why? If an atom has electrons that are farther away from its nucleus, then it is stronger.

**Isotope** - the same element but with a different number of neutrons.

**Bohr concept** of the atom: an atom is most stable when its outer shell is completely filled with electrons.

**Atomic theory:**

- Matter is made up of atoms

- Atoms of the same elements are identical

- Chemical reactions involve either the union or separation of atoms

**Hund's rule:**

**Orbitals** have parallel spins before an orbital is completely filled.

**Electrons** like to enter empty orbitals (empty rooms) before entering a half-filled one.

**Pauli Exclusion Principle** - no two same electrons may occupy any orbital.

**Gram molecular weight** - the mass, or the average weight of one mole of a compound.

**Periodic table and trends**:

Quantum numbers:

P = principle quantum number (N)

A = azimuthal quantum number (l)

M = magnetic quantum number Me

S = spin quantum number Ms

**Problem**

1.
    The number of protons in the nucleus is termed the_____.
2.
    Adding or removing protons_____ the element (changes it to another element).
3.
    The _____ _____ therefore equals the number of protons and neutrons present in the nucleus of the atom.
4.
    What happens when a neutron is added or removed?

**Solution**

1.
    Atomic number
2.
    Transmutes
3.
    Atomic mass
4.
    Forms different isotopes of the same element.

**Ground state** - the condition where the electrons are at their lowest energy levels.

**Electrons** - the same kinetic energy, mass, and speed. Things that we see with electrons: speed of light, wavelength, and frequency.

**Electron configuration** - shows the arrangement of electrons in the atom.

**Orbital types** - the orbitals are the fuzzy spaces in which electrons exist and they come in s, p, d, f.

**Atomic theory** - atoms or groups of atoms join together to form molecules.

**Molecular geometry** - relates to the molecular shapes

**Quantum mechanics** - the blurry picture of the electrons.

**de Broglie's equation** - shows that matter has wavelike properties.

Nature of the **chemical bond** - A chemical bond results from the simultaneous attraction of electrons to two nuclei.

**Exothermic** - releases heat.

**Endothermic** - absorbs heat.

**Bond types** - covalent; double bond; ionic triple; delocalized.

**Covalent bonds** - in a covalent bonded compound, electrons are shared between atoms so that each atom acquires a noble gas configuration.

**Polar covalent** - electrons are unequally shared.

**Non-polar covalent** - electrons are equally shared.

The **shared electron pair** is pulled more strongly to the nucleus of the electro-negative atom.

The **shared electron pair** is equally distributed between the two nuclei sharing the electrons.

The **covalent bond** is not as strong as an ionic bond.

**Covalently bound** molecular substances are:

- 

31

Poor conductors of heat and electricity

- Soft

- Easy to melt and evaporate

- Capable of existing in all three phases (solid, liquid, gas)

**Coordinate covalent bond** - one atom furnishes both of the electrons being shared.

**Network solids** - consist of covalently bonded atoms which continue indefinitely throughout the solid.

- Hardness

- High melting point

- Electrical insulation

- Solid state at room temperature

- Sublimation: the process whereby a solid is converted directly into a gas

**Concepts of:**

- **Ionic solids**

- **Metals**

- **Bonds between molecules**

- **Metallic, ionic and covalent bonding**

- **Percent composition**

- **Empirical formulas**

- **Kinetic theory of gases**

-

- **Chemical kinetics**

- **Activation energy**

- **Half-life**

- **Rate law**

- **Graham's law**

- **Dalton's law**

- **Boyle's law**

- **Charles' law**

- **Hess's law**

- **Law of thermodynamics**

# Organic Chemistry

**I'M NOT SURE WHERE** or when I heard about studying organic chemistry on your own, but I heard it somewhere and tried it. The problem-solving techniques that are developed by taking exams, performing experiments, attending lectures, and studying with classmates all contribute to the learning experience. I memorized the material, but when I took the exam it looked like French to me and I don't speak French. I would not recommend this route.

*DAT tip:* Is it true that guessing Bs on a multiple choice test will give you a higher score? I tried it and the result was better than 20%.

In researching this book I came across an online instructor named *Chad McAllister* of *Coursesaver*. Now this is not an advertisement for him, but I wish that I had his videos to watch when I was going to school. He has a unique way of presenting the information that is entertaining and easy to remember.

**Concepts:**

- **Bonding**

- **Mechanisms**

- **Molecules**

- **Stereochemistry**

- **Acid-base**

- **Aromatic**

- **Synthesis**

# Physics

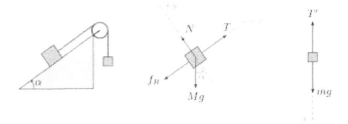

**FOR THOSE OF YOU** who don't love math, physics can be hard. You will learn about force, mass, momentum, wavelengths, velocity, speed of light, gravity, and optics, and will have a chance to use your geometry and trigonometry skills. Many of the laws of physics are expressed in mathematical formulas you may or may not have learned before.

Often times I would wake up in the middle of the night with the answers to my physics problems. My subconscious mind would be working out problems during sleep and many times I would awaken with insight that I had not had before. Yes, physics can be complicated for those who are math challenged.

*Pre-dental tip:* take your math classes in a logical order. Take physics after trigonometry. You will need it for solving the problems.

Although it is not on the DAT, physics is an important tool for the future dentist. You will use concepts of torque, force and energy when prescribing the type of restoration for patients. For example, do you go with a gold or porcelain crown on a posterior case?

**Key words and concepts:**

- **Motion**
- **Acceleration**
- **Falling with gravity**
- **Projectiles**
- **Force and motion**
- **Newton**
- **Gravity**
- **Momentum**
- **Work and energy**
- **Waves**
- **Motion**
- **Sounds**
- **Fluids and solids**
- **Electro**
- **Electric circuits**
- **Light and optics**
- **Spectra**

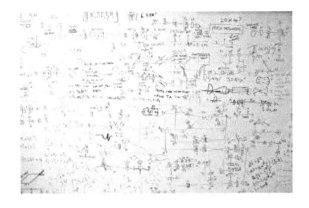

For students who haven't taken physics before this is what a college physics lecture looks like, but don't worry, you'll get used to it.

## Laboratory

**YOUR BIOLOGY, CHEMISTRY, AND PHYSICS** classes will have a lab component that goes along with it. What you can expect in science lab:

# BIOLOGY

In biology lab you will be observing slides, performing experiments on plants and dissecting specimens. Occasionally you will have lab practical exams where you walk around, observe and name what you see. Knowing beforehand how to use a microscope helps as there will be times where you will be working with a microscope in class and in your dental career.

# CHEMISTRY

In chemistry lab you are pretty much on your own. You will be assembling and performing complicated experiments. For example, you may be given a powder with three known chemicals and one unknown. With the use of processes such as heat, chemicals, a centrifuge, filtration and chemical reactions you'll make an educated guess to name your powder. Talking is kept to a minimum, you'll get to know how to light a Bunsen burner and you'll develop the skill to wash instruments quickly and efficiently.

# PHYSICS

In physics lab you most likely will be in a group of your choosing. The power sources have to be built from scratch and experiments conducted where your group will collect data using wavelength, electrical currents and weight, among other things. It's a good idea to make friends with your group in case you have questions on the lab report.

## Other Classes

BY TAKING NON-SCIENCE classes you will have a good chance to raise your GPA. This is a good time for that golf, tennis, or creative writing class you wanted to take. But be careful—I had a swimming teacher who nearly drowned me once a week, and then gave me a C- in the course.

Be a wise manager of your GPA, not a victim. This will be your job—to manage your GPA as high as you can get it, followed by great DAT scores and glowing letters of recommendations by your advisor and professors, and a great essay and interview to match. Be proactive, but be careful not to overcommit on your extracurricular activities.

Keep in mind that you will be ranked according to your math and science GPA, and general GPA. Please read your prospective dental school's website for requirements as each school may be different. Spanish can be helpful when you are treating patients as well as English classes; business classes like marketing, management, and accounting could also help in the future. Some schools may require classes such as microbiology, human anatomy, biochemistry, cell biology, physiology, pathology, endocrinology, statistics, English and sociology. I took a dental science class from a community college which had a dental laboratory program which I felt was worth it.

## Math

FOR THIS GOAL you will encounter a lot of math. From basic math to trigonometry and everything in-between, the science classes revolve around applying the mathematical formulas to the concepts of physics, chemistry and biology.

The math concepts:

- 

    Scientific notation
-

- **Algebra**
- **Fractions**
- **Statistics**
- **Geometry**
- **Percentages - a common DAT subject**
- **Probability - likely on the DAT**

**Common conversions:**

Quart = 32 ounces

Pounds = 16 ounces; 453.59 grams

Inches = 2.54 centimeters

Yard = 3 feet

Meter = 1.0936 yards

1 Kilogram = 1000 grams; 2.2046 pounds

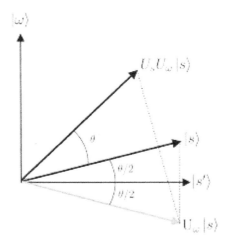

Geometry

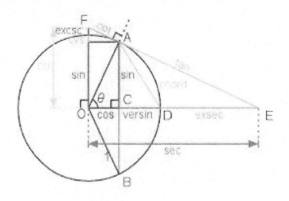

Trigonometry

Basic math, pre-algebra, algebra, geometry, trigonometry, and calculus. A good 6 classes (or three years!) of a subject that I despised in high school. You might as well make friends with math since you will be using it a lot.

*Pre-dental tip:* you will solve word problems in chemistry, physics and on the math section of the DAT.

# CHAPTER FOUR

# The Dental Admission Test (DAT)

**THE DAT** is an exam that uses biology, general chemistry, organic chemistry, perceptual ability, reading comprehension, and quantitative reasoning to compare applicants and is a predictor of how a student will do in dental school. This will be the single most important exam you will take at this stage in your academic career.

The DAT is your chance to shine. You will be compared with all other applicants so you should represent yourself well. The DAT has been in operation since 1950 and began as a paper-and-pencil exam. Today it is computer based. Applicants spend over 300 hours and more than three months to prepare for this important exam.

## INFORMATION

How to apply for the DAT:

www.ada.org where you get a Dentpin (pin number) and download a request form.

Costs: $385 year round

DAT results: $190 for 5 schools, $25 each additional school

Dates: Spring or summer, prior to applying, no later than December 1.

Locations: go to this website for more information www.prometric.com (can be taken on a daily basis).

# DAT SCHEDULE

Optional tutorial: 15 minutes

Survey of the Natural Sciences: 100 questions for 90 minutes

Biology: 40 questions

General Chemistry: 30 questions

Organic Chemistry: 30 questions

Note: There may be changes in the biology sections to focus more on the complex interactions within biological systems.

PAT: (perceptual ability test) 90 questions and 60 minutes

Keyhole: 15 minutes

Top/front/end visualization: 15 minutes

Angle ranking: 15 minutes

Hole punching: 15 minutes

Cube counting: 15 minutes

Pattern folding: 15 minutes

Optional bank: 15 minutes

Reading Comprehension: 50 questions, 60 minutes

3 Essays

Quantitative Reasoning: 40 questions, 45 minutes

Includes: algebra, critical reasoning, fractions, roots, and trigonometry.

Math: 50 questions

Applied Math (word problems): 10 minutes

Note: There may be a reduction in numerical calculations, conversions, geometry, and trigonometry with more emphasis on data analysis, interpretations, sufficiency, quantitative comparison, and probability and statistics.

Optional post-test survey: 15 minutes

Total: 280 questions in 4 hours and 45 minutes. There is a 15-minute optional tutorial break.

Results are given immediately.

It is known that the test makers like to experiment with various types of questions, so the test might be a little different from what you were expecting.

### Learn the material, and then go for speed

What's the secret? Assume that the test is much harder than you think, because it is. I found it to be much harder than any practice test that I took.

# DAT PREPARATION

Study when you are at your freshest. This is an exercise in discipline, endurance and concentration.

New changes: keep up to date on all the latest developments. They are constantly changing the test and experimenting with the materials.

*DAT tip:* my practice tests mirrored my actual scores.

# STUDY TIPS

Learn everything you can about the exam.

Develop a study schedule.

Practice as much as possible: take a lot of practice exams.

Focus on your weak areas.

Give yourself enough time to prepare.

During the last week take an exam a day.

Learn the material then . . . develop speed.

Stick to a routine.

Prepare hard and think positive.

Get test-ready by taking a lot of tests for stamina. You want to be relaxed, confident, and in good mental, physical and spiritual shape to perform at your optimum best.

*DAT tip:* try to construct your own questions so you can think like a test maker.

# DAT RESOURCES

AP biology books
Barron's Guide to the DAT
CliffsNotes for biology, chemistry, physics, math
Crack the DAT/PAT software: math, reading, science
Coursesaver: Chad's' McAllister's videos are highly recommended (G-Chem, O-Chem)
High Yield
DAT Achiever: 7 full-length practice exams
DAT Cracker
DAT Destroyer: great reviews
DAT Gold Standard
DAT-Prep.com
DAT Q-Vault
DAT Secrets
DAT Top Score Pro-CD
Kaplan: good for a general review, preparation centers
Kaplan Blue Book (available on amazon.com)
Pre-DDS
Princeton
YouTube videos
TOP Score
Speed-reading books
Studentdoctor.net
National Learning Corporation
Betz Publishing
Full exam tests for your final review

ASDAnet.org is the definitive source of dental information from prep, planning, tips, support, how to guides, etc. There's a fee.

I'm amazed at the amount of DAT materials out there today. That being said, how do you know which one to use? The *Student Doctor Network* forum is a great source of support and information. The free sharing of DAT tips is one of the best online and I would start off my DAT research there. There are videos of successful students describing their DAT experiences and how they prepared and their reviews of the various companies. The website www.dentaldat.com was is excellent source of information regarding tips and advice.

# DAT/Biology

**THERE IS ONLY** so much they can ask. Study your weaknesses and keep squeezing your notes.

- **The Five Kingdoms**
- **Ecological systems**
- **Cell Biology**
- **Mendel's genetics**
- **Prokaryotes and eukaryotes**
- **The three germ layers**
- **Pancreas**
- **Digestion**
- **Pituitary gland**
- **Kidney**
- **Glands and hormones**
- **Enzymes**
- **Muscles**
- **Brain functions**
-

- **Bioenergetics**

- **Biosyntheses**

- **Developmental biology**

- **Population biology**

- **Evolution and comparative anatomy**

*DAT biology tip*: the exam was mostly on human things. Five questions came from bioenergetics and photosynthesis, embryology, energetics, the Krebs cycle, respiration, depolarization and permeability.

*DAT tip:* the heart is a common exam subject.

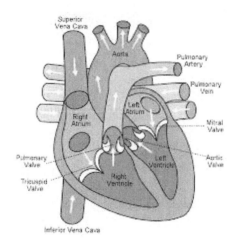

## PULMONARY CIRCULATION AND SYSTEMIC CIRCULATION

The heart is divided into four chambers. The right atrium, right ventricle, left atrium, and left ventricle.

**Heart terms:**

**Alveolus** - is the site of gas exchange.

**Anterior vena cava** - responsible for conducting deoxygenated blood from the upper part of the body to the right atrium of the heart.

**Posterior vena cava** - the large vein that receives blood from the lower extremities.

**Superior vena cava** - the large vein that returns the blood to the heart from the head, neck and arms.

**Blood** - is re-oxygenated in the lungs.

There are **pulmonary arteries** (on the right side) and **pulmonary veins** on the left.

**Pulmonary artery** - is where blood flows away from the heart.

**Pulmonary veins** - return blood to the heart.

**Aorta** - is the largest main artery of the human body.

The **artery** - is a thick, rigid muscle layer that doesn't collapse easily. It carries blood away from the heart.

The **vein** - is less rigid, softer, has weak walls, and receives blood from the capillaries where it returns it to the heart.

**Capillaries** - have one layer and are very small and thin.

The human **heartbeat** - is started in the sinoatrial node.

**Problem**

The ___ sends oxygenated blood from the lungs to the body.

    a.
        Superior vena cava
    b.
        Right atrium
    c.
        Left ventricle
    d.
        Descending aorta
    e.
        Aorta

**Solution**

The answer is E. The aorta carries oxygenated blood away from the heart.

Blood flows from the superior vena cava to the right atrium.

The right atrium sends blood to the right ventricle.

The left ventricle supplies blood to the aorta.

**Problem**

Draw the heart and label the:

    a)
        Right atrium
    b)
        Left atrium
    c)
        Right ventricle
    d)
        Left ventricle

**Problem**

Where is blood pressure the highest?

    a)
        Capillaries
    b)
        Sinoatrial node
    c)
        Left ventricle, systole
    d)
        Left ventricle, diastole
    e)
        Pulmonary artery

**Solution**

Answer is C, the left ventricle, systole. Diffusion of materials in and out of the circulatory system takes place in the capillaries. The sinoatrial node is where contraction takes place.

Diastole is where the heart refills with blood. Blood pressure is low and the pulmonary artery carries deoxygenated blood to the lungs.

**Problem**

47

What conditions would you NOT expect to be met in the Hardy-Weinberg Principle?

a)

Random mating

b)

No migration

c)

Mutations

d)

A large population

e)

Free flow of genes

**Solution**

Answer is C. There are no mutations or migrations, mating must be random, the population must be large and isolated, and there must be no natural selection pressure. The Hardy-Weinberg principle describes what happens to the frequencies of alleles and genotypes in a hypothetical population of ideal reproducing organisms.

**Problem**

**According to the Hardy-Weinberg Principle what conditions must be met for equilibrium?**

a)

Large population

b)

Random mating

c)

No mutations or migrations

d)

Sexually reproducing organisms.

e)

All

**Solution**

Answer is E. According to the Hardy-Weinberg Principle all these conditions must be met.

*DAT tip:* there may be equations to calculate. Sometimes it might be a good idea to wait until the end to do the time consuming questions.

**Kidney terms:**

**Bladder** - is where urine is collected.

**Bowman's capsule** - cup-shaped, around the glomerulus of each nephron of the kidneys.

**Collecting tubule** - the part of the nephron that collects from the distal and discharges to the pelvis of the kidney.

**Distal convoluted tubule** - a part of the nephron (kidney) between the loop of Henle and the collecting duct system.

**Glomerulus** - relative to the kidney a collection of vessels or fibers.

**Kidney** - removes waste from the body. The kidney is involved in filtration, secretion and resorption.

**Loop of Henle** - in relation to the kidneys, it's the lower loop in the nephron.

**Medulla** - the central tissue of the kidney and the adrenal glands.

**Nephron** - the excretory unit of the kidney.

**Proximal convoluted tubule** - the portion of the duct system of the nephron of the kidneys.

**Renal artery** - supplies the kidney with blood.

**Renal vein** - drains the kidneys.

**Ureter** - tubes that send urine from the kidney to the bladder.

**Urethra** - discharges urine, a tube that travels from the urinary bladder to elimination.

**Krebs cycle** - a sequence of reactions by which living cells generate energy.

**Respiration (cellular)** - the conversion of oxygen into energy.

**Photosynthesis** - the process of converting light energy to chemical energy and storing it in the bonds of sugar.

**Ecosystems** - a community of living organisms.

**Dihybrid cross** - Mendel's genetics. May be combined with probability, but you probably won't have time to make a Punnet square.

**Liver** - plays a role in metabolism, digestion, detoxification and elimination.

You may be asked questions from **bioenergetics, photosynthesis** and **blood clotting.**

**Sperm/reproduction** - meiosis and mitosis.

**Meiosis** - when two cells divide into four daughter nuclei.

**Embryology** - deals with the formation, development and structure of living things.

**Fetus** - later stage of development.

**Mesenteric tissue** - tissue that attaches organs to the body wall.

**Homeostasis** - the tendency of a cell to regulate a balance or equilibrium with the internal environment to the environmental changes.

**Problem**

What muscles are not part of the muscles system of the head?

a)
   Frontalis
b)
   Temporalis
c)
   Occipitalis
d)
   Masseter
e)
   Trapezius

**Solution**

Answer is E. The frontalis, oribicularis oculi, zygomaticus, orbicularis oris, masseter, temporalis and occipitalis are part of the skeletal muscles of the head.

The trapezius muscle lies near the shoulder blade.

**Problem**

What teeth are used for chewing and grinding?

    a)
        Anteriors

    b)
        Centrals

    c)
        Cuspids

    d)
        Posterior

    e)
        All of the above

**Solution**

Answer is D, the posterior teeth. The anteriors are used to tear food. The centrals and cuspids are part of the anterior teeth. The posterior teeth (the molars and bicuspids) are used for chewing and grinding food.

**Problem**

Of the following what are associated with digestion?

    a)
        Loop of Henle

    b)
        Salivary glands

    c)
        Sinoatrial node

    d)
        Prolactin

    e)
        Posterior pituitary

**Solution**

Answer is B. The salivary glands produce saliva which begins the process of starch digestion. Saliva contains ptyalin (salivary amylase) which digests starch to maltose.

The loop of Henle is associated with kidney functions.

The sinoartial node is where the heartbeat is initiated.

Prolactin stimulates milk secretion by mammary glands.

The posterior pituitary is the storage organ for hormones produced by the hypothalamus.

**Teeth:**

1.
   The incisors and canines are used in_____ and _____ food.
2.
   The pre-molars and molars have _____ surfaces for _____.
3.
   Humans have _____ teeth.
4.
   The exposed part of the tooth has a very hard covering called_____.
5.
   _____ sets of salivary glands supply the mouth with saliva.
6.
   Saliva contains the enzyme_____.

**Answers:**

1.
   Cutting and tearing
2.
   Grinding, chewing
3.
   32
4.
   Enamel
5.
   Three
6.
   Amylase

**Problem**

Which of the following is not part of the digestive system?

a)

　　Liver

b)

　　Stomach

c)

　　Esophagus

d)

　　Appendix

e)

　　Heart

## Solution

Answer is E. All the choices are part of the digestive systems except the heart. The heart is part of the circulatory system.

## Problem

Bile is produced in the

a)

　　Liver

b)

　　Kidneys

c)

　　Pancreas

d)

　　Gall bladder

e)

　　Small intestine

## Solution

Answer is A. Bile is produced in the liver.

## Problem

Which of the following is part of the kidney?

a)

　　Aorta

b)

　　Capillaries

c)

d)

Veins

Superior vena cava

e)

Loop of Henle

**Solution**

Answer is E. The aorta, capillaries, veins and superior vena cava are associated with the circulatory system. The loop of Henle is part of the kidney.

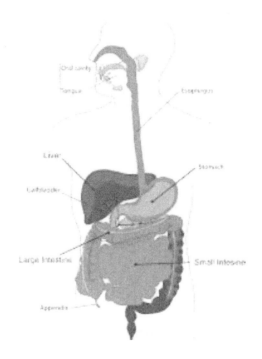

**Digestion:**

**Mouth** - 32 teeth.

**Pharynx** - the epiglottis closes off the passageway during swallowing.

**Esophagus** - food is pushed down by peristaltic waves.

**Stomach** - three major functions are storage, mechanical breakdown, and chemical breakdown.

**Small intestine** - where most of the digestion and absorption of nutrients takes place.

**Large intestine** - leaves a semi-solid fecal mass.

**Rectum** - holding site until elimination.

**Anus** - terminal sphincter.

**Liver** - the producer of bile.

**Pancreas** - produces enzymes that are secreted in the duodenum.

**Gall bladder** - stores bile which assists in digestion and breakdown of fats.

**Esophagus** - is a muscular tube.

**Pharynx** - the area between the mouth and the trachea. The presence of food stimulates swallowing.

**Duodenum** - the first part of the small intestine. Bile, pancreatic and digestive enzymes occur here.

**Peristaltic waves** - food is pushed down by a series of circular muscular contractions.

## Problem

The glands in the stomach produce:

a)
    Hydrochloric acid
b)
    Pepsin
c)
    Rennin
d)
    A and B
e)
    All the above

## Solution

Answer is D. The gastric gland in the stomach produces hydrochloric acid and the enzymes pepsin and rennin. Pepsin digests proteins to peptones. While Rennin curdles milk and delays its passage through the stomach.

What is **natural selection**? It relates to genetics and heredity.

**Darwin's theory of evolution** - a theory that claims that all species have developed from other species.

What are the most advanced phyla of the **animal kingdom**? Animalia.

**Phylum** - a classification, above class and below kingdom.

**RNA** - has a phosphate sugar backbone

The insertion of a single nucleotide base in a cell's **DNA** results in a frame shift mutation, a genetic mutation relating to genetics.

**Photosynthetic organism** - organisms that rely on photosynthesis; examples are green plants.

What is an example of a **prokaryote**? Bacteria, they don't posses a membrane-bound nucleus. (An example is e-coli.)

*DAT tip:* what are the differences between prokaryotes and eukaryotes?

**Prokaryotes** = bacteria

**Eukaryotes** = plant and animals

What does the **mitochondrion** do? It produces energy through respiration.

The site of the **Krebs cycle** - reactions in living cells related to proteins and fatty acids.

**Electron transport** - a group of compounds that pass the electron via redox reactions.

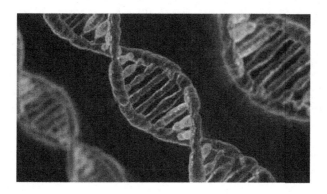

**DNA** is double stranded with a double helix structure. It looks like a ladder where sugars and phosphate groups are linked to form the rungs.

The **DNA** in action - if we look into the nucleus on a cell we would find DNA plus protein which are chromosomes.

**Nucleus**: DNA + protein = Chromosomes

**Nucleotides** are the building blocks of DNA and RNA.

The **RNA** is a single chain in the form of a helix.

These **nucleotides** are made up of a sugar or phosphate group or a base. The base pairs are:

A= adenine

T= thymine

G= guanine

C= cytosine

Adenine pairs with thymine

Guanine pairs with cytosine

A+T and G+C. The base pair varies with species but is constant in a species and doesn't change with diet, environment or age.

**DNA replication** - is the process in which DNA is copied. It is a template for new RNA to produce.

Recognize the difference between a strand of DNA and RNA.

**RNA** is single-stranded with a ribose sugar backbone. Base pairs of ACGU; mRNA, tRNA, rRNA.

In general **RNA** is made from DNA. The double helix of the DNA unwinds so that the RNA can get access to it.

**RNA** differs in structure from DNA in three ways. First, it has a ribose sugar versus a deoxyribose sugar. Second, it is made of uracil, instead of thymine, and finally, it is single-stranded compared with the double strands of DNA.

Cycle of Nutrients in an **ecosystem:**

Water

Temperature

Solar

Oxygen

Solids

A general characteristic of an adult echinoderm is radial symmetry and tube feet.

**Monera** - they are prokaryotes (no nucleus) and unicellular.

**Protista** - single-celled organisms (eukaryotes) unicellular.

**Fungi** - heterotrophic organisms (eukaryotes) multicellular.

**Plantae** - plants and multicellular.

**Animalia** - animals, multicellular.

**Autotrophs** - can produce their own food by the use of light through photosynthesis.

**Photosynthesis** - the role of light is to split the water molecule.

Chlorophyll + sunlight = food

$CO_2$ + $H_2O$ produces food

**Heterotrophs** - can't produce their own energy. This is the case with most bacteria, all fungi, and animals.

**First Law of Thermodynamics** - energy balances out.

**Second Law is the Entropy Law** - systems progress from order to disorder.

Know the parts of the **cell** - the glycocalyx, lysosome, rough endoplasmic reticulum, golgi complex, mitochondrion, chromosomes, and nucleolus.

**Vacuole** - a space within the cytoplasm that is filled with medium whose functions include secretion, excretion, storage, and digestion.

**Nuclear membrane** - has pores and is a double-layered lipid bilayer.

**Nucleolus** - serves as the site of ribosome synthesis and assembly.

**Endoplasmic reticulum** - a network of tubular membranes.

**Microtubules** - responsible for movement.

**Centriole** - a small set of microtubules arranged in a specific way.

**Mitochondrion** - an organelle found in most cells that produces energy through respiration.

The **cell** contains nucleic acid, proteins, lipids, and polysaccharides.

What are the three ways a substance can pass through a **plasma membrane?** Through pores, dissolving or diffusing through the membrane, and finally by binding to a carrier protein and being carried across.

**Phospholipids** - are the building blocks of cell membranes.

**Lysosomes** - membrane-enclosed organelles capable of breaking down via enzymes.

The **nucleus** - contains the genetic material present in eukaryotic cells.

**Chromosomes** - contains most of the DNA.

**Bacteria** divide by binary fission.

A **virus:**

- Is a nucleic molecule with a protein coat
- Needs a host to multiply, it can't carry out metabolically
- Is not living until it invades a host cell
- Can stay in the crystallized state for a long time
- Reproduces by invading a host cell which causes the host to produce more DNA.

**Problem**

The characteristics of viruses are:

a)
They are important in communicable diseases

b)
They provide insight into evolution

c)
They can be used to help fight diseases

d)
They are important for understanding normal cells

e)
All of the above

**Solution**

The answer is E. The understanding of how viruses work is important in microbiology and to understanding how to diagnose diseases.

They need a host to multiply as viruses do not carry out processes outside of the host. Bacteriophages inject their nucleic acid into bacterial cells.

**Parasympathetic nervous system** - the rest response of the involuntary nervous system.

**Sympathetic nervous system** - stimulates the "fight-or-flight" response.

# DAT/General Chemistry

**HOW CAN** you perform well in this area? First go for understanding, then go for speed and practice under test simulations. I would review my weaknesses day and night and do as many problems as possible. It's like running a marathon. You have to build endurance for it.

The **atom** is made up of protons, neutrons, and electrons.

**Atoms** transfer, share or lose electrons.

The **nucleus** is central and highly concentrated.

Sometimes the **mass number** is referred to as atomic mass.

**Electrons** are moving fast. The farther away the electrons are from the nucleus, the more potential energy they possess.

**Hund's rule** - orbitals have parallel spins before an orbital is completely filled.

**Endothermic** - absorbs energy from its environment.

Types of **chemical bonds** - ionic, covalent, polar covalent.

**Covalent bonds** - in a covalent bonded compound, electrons are shared between atoms so that each atom acquires a noble gas configuration.

The **covalent bond** is not as strong as an ionic bond.

Covalently bound molecular substances are:

- Poor conductors of heat and electricity

- Soft

- Easy to melt and evaporate

- Capable of existing in all three phases (solid, liquid, gas)

**Coordinate covalent bond** - one atom furnishes both of the electrons being shared.

**Non-polar covalent** - electrons that are equally shared are called a pure covalent bond.

**Polar** covalent - electrons are unequally shared.

The shared **electron pair** is pulled more strongly to the nucleus of the electro-negative atom.

The shared **electron pair** is equally distributed between the two nuclei sharing the electrons.

**Hydrogen bonding** involves the electrostatic interaction of a hydrogen atom in one species with an electronegative atom in another species.

**Van der Waals forces** - weak forces of attraction between nonpolar (equally distributed) molecules be they dipole-dipole or London forces.

**Network solids** consist of covalently bonded atoms which continue indefinitely throughout the solid:

- Hardness
- High melting point
- Electrical insulation
- Solid state at room temperature

**Ionization energy** - An **ion** is an atom with an electrical charge due to the gain or loss of one or more electrons. It is the amount of energy that an isolated atom in the ground electronic state must absorb to discharge an electron.

**Electronegativity** - the measure of the tendency of an atom to attract a bonding pair of electrons.

**Size** - atomic radius

**Molecular weights** - the molecular weight is related to the mass of a molecule. It is one mole of a substance.

**Chemical formulas** - expressions which represent the number and types of atoms in a molecule.

**Temperature and pressure**

**Density**

**Specific heat**

**Gases, liquids, and solids**

**Changes in state** - it is harder to compress a liquid to a solid than a gas to a liquid because the molecules in a liquid are already close together.

**Dalton's law of partial pressures** - determines the individual pressures of each gas in a mixture.

**Ideal gas equations**

**Equations and computations**

**Oxidation**

**Nuclear chemistry** - deals with the radioactive and nuclear processes. (see below)

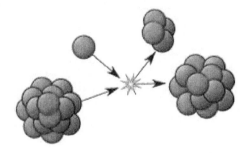

**Thermochemistry** - the study of energy and heat.

**Electrochemistry** - the study of electricity and chemical reactions.

**Organic compounds** - compounds that contain carbon.

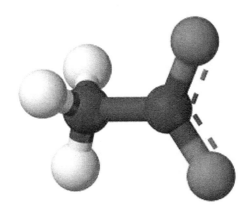

Acetate

Carbons = Black

Hydrogen = Grey

Oxygen = Red

Calculate the **concentration** of one ion.

Calculate the **solubility** from Ksp.

**Predicting precipitate** and **calculating concentration** of ions left in solution.

**Common ions effect**

**Ph and solubility**

**Calculate concentration**

**Calculate solubility**

**Predict:**

**Common ions**

**Ph and solubility**

Why do they include a periodic chart? Is it because there will be a question on it?

**Periodic table trends:**

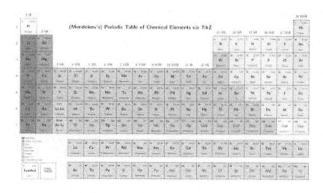

**Periodic table** - names, electrons, oxidation, trends, orbitals, isotopes, and compounds:

- Nonmetals

- Transition metals

- Nontransition metals

- Periodic table to predict an element - gains electrons, reducing agent, oxidizing agent

- Positions on the periodic table

- Oxide and base

- Melting points

- Is this element radioactive?

**Use the periodic table to predict the electronic configuration** - as we go across the periodic table the number of electrons increases as well as the valence shell electrons. As they get farther away from the nucleus the size increases.

**Reactive metals** combine with **reactive nonmetals** to produce ionic compounds.

**Active metals, transition elements, active nonmetals, inert gases.**

**Electrons** in its outermost energy levels

**Atomic radius** - measure of the size of an atom.

**Periodic law** - many of the properties of the elements tend to reoccur in a systematic way.

## Problems

The farther away an electron is from the nucleus makes it:

a)
   Stronger
b)
   Weaker
c)
   Stable
d)
   Unstable
e)
   All the answers can be right

## Solution

Answer is A.

Electrons are moving fast. The farther away the electrons are from the nucleus, the more potential energy they possess. Why? Because the *separation* of positive and negative changes is greater. Put another way, if an atom has electrons that are farther away from its nucleus, then it is stronger.

If you were to add or remove protons the element would change. Adding or subtracting neutrons changes the isotopes.

**Isotopes** - same elements with equal numbers of protons, but a different number of electrons.

**Sublimation** - the process whereby a solid is converted directly into a gas.

**Ionic solids**

**Metals**

**Bonds between molecules**

66

## Metallic, ionic and covalent bonding

**Gibbs** - thermodynamic potential of work obtainable at a constant temperature and pressure.

**Graham's law of diffusion** - the rate at which gases diffuse is inversely proportional to the square root of their densities.

**Kinetic theory** is a gas with a large number of atoms, which are in a constant random motion:

- Occupies no volume
- Purely elastic collisions
- Temperature increase causes kinetic energy increase
- No interparticle forces

The **rate of a reaction** seeks to account for the rates of the reactions and to describe the conditions and mechanisms by which reactions proceed.

What are the factors that affect the **rates of reactions**?

- The nature of the reactions
- Ionic reactions in any solution
- Direct combinations
- Reactions are slow
- Concentrations of the reactants
- Temperatures
- Reaction mechanism
- Catalysis

**Reaction orders:**

**Chemical reactions** are classified on a kinetic basis by reaction order.

The **reaction rate** is influenced by the presence of the reactants under a given set of conditions.

First order: rate = K [A]

Second order: rate = K [A] 2

*DAT tip:* a common question is to determine the order of the reaction with some information given. It's a math calculation. Be careful as common errors will be provided as answers.

**Calculations** - my experience with the DAT was that it was the same as the practice tests, except I needed more time. There was a rate law question, oxidation, theory, and computations. Of all the areas doing calculations was the most time consuming.

**Enthalpy** - thermodynamic potential.

**Kinetics**

Know how to work with the **rate law**.

**Potential energy** - the energy possessed by a body.

**Activation energy** - the minimum energy needed to cause a chemical reaction.

The **catalyst** acts by providing a new reaction pathway with lower activation energy and thus a larger rate constant.

A **catalyst** speeds up a chemical reaction by increasing the rates of both the forward and the reverse reactions. The catalyst doesn't affect the final amounts of reactant and products, just the rate of speed.

**Rates:**

- 
   The order of each reactant
- 
   Rate constant
- 
   Mechanism of reaction
-

Arrhenius equation: temperature dependence of reaction rates

- Collision state theory: reactant particles must collide for a reaction

What are the areas of **kinetics**? The rate of the reactions, orders, the rate constant, what happens after a collision, the Arrhenius equation and carbon dating.

**Half-life** - the amount of time required for one-half of a sample to decay.

**Properties of solution**

**Stoichiometry**

**Acid-base:**

An **acid** is a proton donor and a base is a proton acceptor.

**Acids** donate protons, and bases accept them.

**Ph** is a measure of the acidity of an aqueous solution.

**Weak acids and bases** dissociate partially in water.

**Strong acids and bases** completely dissociate in aqueous solutions.

The majority of **acid and bases** are weak.

The **Bronsted-Lowry** theory states that an acid is a substance that can donate a proton, and a base is a substance that can accept a proton.

**Molality** - moles of solute/Kg or 100 grams of solvent

**Molarity** - mole of solute/liter of solution

**Normality** - equivalents solute/liter of solution

**Henderson-Hasselbalch** can be used to calculate the pH of a buffer solution.

A **buffer** solution suppresses pH changes when acid or base is added.

Properties of **gases**

**Boyle's law**

**Ideal gas law**

**Ideal gas equation** - relates to pressure, volume, gas and temperature.

**Ideal gas equation**: **PV=nRT**

P = pressure

V = volume

N = number

R = rate

T = temperature

If the temperature increases, the volume increases or if the pressure increases, the volume decreases (like the pressure cooker).

**Gasses** are compressible.

**Combined gas law equation** - a combination of Charles' law, Boyle's law, and the gas equation.

**Density of an ideal gas** - used to calculate the density for an ideal gas.

**Le Chatelier's principle** - if a system at equilibrium is disturbed then the reaction proceeds in a direction to relieve the stress.

**Kinetic theory** - a gas is a large number of atoms:

- Occupies no volume
- Purely elastic collisions
- A temperature increase causes a kinetic theory increase
- No interparticle forces (no attractive or repulsive forces)

*DAT tip:* the best way to prepare for the DAT is to do a lot of review questions, problems and practice exams. Making review notes and squeezing them as you go along is a technique that has been used for many years.

# DAT/Organic Chemistry

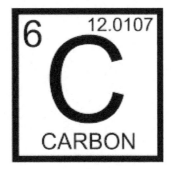

**ORGANIC CHEMISTRY** is the field of chemistry of **carbon compounds** in combination with **oxygen** and **hydrogen** as well as other elements.

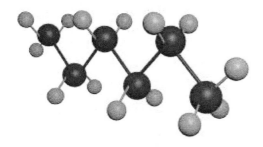

Hexane molecule

Ball and stick representation

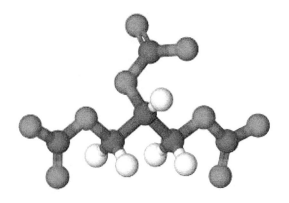

R = 5'-deoxyadenosyl, Me, OH, CN

A B12 molecule

Line angle representation of a molecule

A molecule of Nitroglycerin

Ball and stick style representation of a molecule

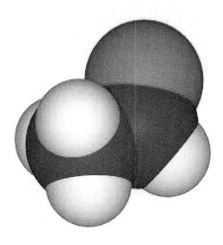

Acetaldehyde

Space filling style representation of a molecule

Carbon = Black

Oxygen = Red

Hydrogen = Grey

Nitrogen = Blue

Sulfur = Yellow

Fluorine, Chlorine = Green

**Bonding**

**Mechanisms**

**Chemical and chemical properties**

**Reactions**

**Grignard** reagent formed by the reaction of magnesium metal with alkyl or alkenyl halides.

**Aldol condensation** - an organic chemistry carbon reaction.

**Claisne condensation** - similar to aldol condensation.

**Diels-Alder reaction** - a famous organic chemistry reaction.

**Isomerism** - molecules with the same molecular formula, but with a different arrangement of atoms.

**Know the common reactions and the nomenclature names**

**Stereoisomers**

**Cyclohexane** - interesting shapes from a boat to a chair.

**Functional groups** - atoms in a molecule that participate in reactions.

**Huckel rule** - predicts whether a planar ring molecule will have aromatic properties.

**Common oxidizing agents**

**Molality, molarity, normality**

Organic compounds are distinguished by the ability of the carbon atoms to make chains. These chains can be branched or unbranched, or made into closed rings. A closed ring is called **crystallization.**

There are four divisions of **organic compounds**

1.
   Aliphatic
2.
   Alicyclic
3.
   Aromatic
4.
   Heterocyclic

**Aliphatic compounds** are carbon chains that are branched or unbranched.

**Alicyclic compounds** have one or more rings.

**Aromatic compounds** are benzene rings that are closed and contain six atoms.

**Hetrocyclic compounds** are closed rings in which one of the elements is other than carbon.

## Organic families

**Homologues** - a family of compounds of increasing molecular weight.

**Hydrocarbons** - compounds that contain hydrogen and carbon.

**Paraffin family** - these compounds belong to the aliphatic division and are said to be saturated.

**Benzene family** - the aromatic hydrocarbons form families in two ways:

1.
    Adding organic radicals to a benzene ring.
2.
    By adding benzene rings.

**Carbohydrate family** - these are chains containing carbon, hydrogen and oxygen. A carbohydrate is made up of sugar and starch.

**Substituted organic compounds** - adding other elements and groups into compounds.

## Organic analysis

## Nomenclature

## Names of alkanes:

## Methane

## Ethane

## Propane

## Butane

## Pentane

## Hexane

## Heptane

## Octane

## Nonane

**Decane**

**IUPAC rules**

**Stereochemistry**

**Isomerism**

**Acidity and basic**

**Ortho**

**OP activating**

**Meta deactivating group**

**Halogens and their exceptions**

# Reading Comprehension

**THE READING SECTION** of the DAT is an important predictor of success in dental school as it tests memory and comprehension. One thing that I found helpful was reading speed-reading books.

## Experiment

You read better when you know what you are reading for. Read the questions before answering them.

## Reading with a purpose

1.
    Read the first paragraph first.
2.
    Make a mind map of paragraph topics.
3.
    Read questions.
4.
    Read fast.
5.
    Answer the questions.

Why do they want dental students to be able to map passages? Is it so you can compartmentalize, organize, store and use knowledge?

## Focus and reasoning

*DAT tips:*

Read the first sentence of each paragraph.

Practice using the dry board.

Don't move your lips when you read, it slows you down.

Organize the information: map it.

Rapid reading is the best way to tackle it.

Experiment with what works best for you.

It's very important to develop this skill and to score high.

Reading science-related materials to get a "feel" for the science information.

## SAMPLE

## Starting Your Dental Business

In my opinion, an entrepreneur doesn't need an MBA to be successful. What's more important is previous experience in starting and running a business, a strong work ethic, and experience in your industry, ability to delegate to professionals (CPA, lawyers, and consultants), the ability to lead and train, the ability to focus on one thing at a time, and the flexibility and wisdom to find your niche. Another important thing is to manage your sales force and to keep your marketing department running.

It's important to get good mentors who will teach you. A good team will expand your skills, help with decision making, expand networks, help in marketing and raising money, share in technology, and will make the experience easier.

The MBA degree trains managers of business. The MBA has the ability to manage, sell, promote, and utilize business functions valuable in a business. They have to deal with what is happening today and progress towards future goals like everyone else.

If you have an MBA some companies may be impressed by your credentials and may offer you special discounts, but you still have to prove you are worthy of their belief and trust.

Sometimes an MBA can hurt your chances of success. After completing my MBA I thought it was the end of school. It was only the beginning. When starting a business there's much to learn, from locating suppliers, finding customers, networking, accounting and invoicing software, to being self-disciplined.

Are you confident because you have a master's degree? Not in the entrepreneurial world. This is another world. This is like the first day of school.

As you progress, you may realize that business school didn't prepare you for this. While in school, you felt you could take on any business and turn it into a success.

What you learned in business school did not prepare you for entrepreneurship. It's hard work. There's a steep learning curve. You will do labor. A lot of time should be spent in sales. This will be a real-world Ph.D. There will be mistakes. You'll learn things about yourself you didn't know. You may lose friends along the journey. Make your failures small and manageable and learn to analyze them.

Having MBA classmates can hurt your chances of success. Imagine this. You will spend time debating which accounting software to use. People want to work with software they know. Some may question your commitment and will impose their goals on the business. They will shout, panic, and insult you. The MBA degree is known for big money, and most startups are small. We had three MBAs in a small business commonly started by a trade person. No one wanted to water plants or throw out the trash.

Starting your own business is not like business school. Guess who throws out the trash? It might be you. Do you want to pay someone to do things you can do yourself? It's probably not a good idea to pay someone for things you can do yourself.

In school the answers are in the books. Every question has an answer. In this business you will manage disrespectful employees who question your knowledge and experience, and you may run out of money.

I was so confident my business plan would work. I was confused why my partners didn't want to read it. The "plan" was granted an honors grade and was in the school library. Reading it ten years later shows how inaccurate it can be. The business plan should be revised at least once a year.

If anything can be learned from this experience it would be to keep focused. But don't let it limit you from working with others that your business plan didn't cover. Sometimes a client or competitor will create an opportunity that you didn't consider.

What works today may not work tomorrow. Things change quickly with technology, regulations, laws, taxes, and competition. Be prepared to be flexible if things are not going your way. Look for opportunities that have good economics, ability to raise prices with inflation, a growing industry, no robotics, no trend towards outsourcing overseas and consolidation. If your industry is experiencing rapidly changing technology, complacency may put you out of business. Your business plan may be good for a few weeks to a month if lucky. Generally it restricts when you need to be researching, testing, and experimenting. It keeps you focused, but can hold you back from testing and trying things. It has a tendency to confine you. Reality check . . . no one cares about your business plan . . . except you.

You must assemble a great team. Everything has to progress at the same time to get ahead. It's impossible to move an entire business according to the business plan by yourself. You have to raise capital and some mistakes will be made. A common mistake is to start too many businesses before one is profitable. But if the main business isn't working you need plan B to survive.

1.

How long does it take for a business to break even?

A.

One year

B.

Two years

C.

Three years

D.

Four years

E.

None of the above

2.

Of the following, what may put you out of business?

A.

Regulations

B.

Rapidly changing technology

C.

Taxes

D.

Competition

E.

All of the above

3.

Having MBA classmates can help:

A.

Some of the time

B.

Never

C.

All of the time

D.

Both A and B

E.

None of the above

4.

The business plan in the passage was:

A.

The thing that guided the business to success

B.

Granted an honors grade

C.

Placed in the library

D.

All of the above

E.

None of the above

5.

The author states that the business can be a:

A.

Real world Ph.D.

B.

Learning example

C.

Way to make a living

D.

None of the above

E.

All of the above

6.

With which of the following statements would the author of the passage agree?

A.

Business plans are a way to solve all business problems.

B.

Having an MBA is very useful when starting a business.

C.

It is best to start several businesses and to keep what is working.

D.

The most effective way to be successful is to assemble a great team.

E.

MBA classmates can help in the success of a business.

7.

It is important to have mentors because they can:

A.

Expand your skills.

B.

Help with financing.

C.

Give you good advice.

D.

Loan you their employees

E.

All of the above

Answers:

1.

E

2.
   E
3.
   D
4.
   D
5.
   E
6.
   D
7.
   E

**Creating a mind map**

First of all, we want to know *what* we are reading for and in reading the first paragraph we can tell this is about business.

If we then map out the reading section by writing the topics of each paragraph we can have a better idea where we can find the answers.

If we go to the questions we can see it's going to be about: the break-even point; things that put you out of business; MBA/MBA classmates, the business plan; description of business; and mentors.

For example:

The first paragraph is about entrepreneurs and MBAs.

The second (short one) is about mentors, which is what question number seven is asking.

We can do a quick scan and see that the *break-even question* is not going to be easy to find and we can continue our map.

Once our map is made we can look for the answers to the questions in the mapped off paragraphs.

*DAT tip*: these questions are to be answered quickly and this is an active reading exercise. The more you practice the better you will get. You should practice this skill every day until your test.

# Reading takes daily practice and hard work

Testing:

- Reading comprehension

- Analytical reasoning

- Logical reasoning

Why? Admissions want to know that you can read with understanding and insight on material similar to what is found in dental school.

# SAMPLE

## Matching a Pre-Existing Central Crown

One the hardest things a dental technician can do is to match a ceramic central crown to another crown. Most of the time it has been made by a different dental technician and to duplicate someone else's style goes above and beyond the regular technician's work. The technician must duplicate the mesial, distal, lingual and facial surfaces as well as consider the line angles, gingival tissue, age of the patient, and the condition of the teeth.

The materials to consider when planning a ceramic crown that is matched to another existing crown is the type of porcelain that was previously used. Porcelain powders vary and these differences are magnified when dealing with a front tooth. Also, consideration must be taken into the type of restoration that is being replaced. What type of margin was used on the crown? Was there a porcelain butt margin? Was it a regular PFM, a pressable crown, or a zirconia or alumina crown?

The problem in matching a central crown is that it is prominent and central to one's appearance. Most people notice the central more than any other tooth. The adult human has 32 teeth in the natural arch, but the #8 and #9 are prominent when working in cosmetic dentistry. The central tooth has three parts that we must distinguish and they are the gingival third, the middle third and the incisal third.

Some patients have developed psychological issues regarding their #8 and #9 central crowns. They may have suffered trauma to their teeth during an early age and lived with a discolored tooth. Others may have been the unfortunate victim of a badly matched crown and didn't realize there is such a thing as a custom shade. Later, as adults, they can be extremely sensitive to the appearance of their new crowns. Some of these patients may need extra attention when they are having their crowns replaced.

The different types of ceramic materials that exist today are multiplying rapidly. In the past there were one or two major porcelain manufactures that controlled the market; today that number has increased exponentially. There are high-temperature porcelains, low-fusing porcelains, large and fine grained porcelains. Extra care must be given to the surface texture of crowns, from a natural unglazed finish or a glazed finish, to a glazed and polished finish.

The success of replacing a central crown takes the collaboration of the dental team which starts and ends with the dentist. Communication is important and high-quality pictures can aid in the sharing of data regarding color. Issues of thickness need to be carefully managed by the dentist. The dental lab must be available to see the patient to address tooth form and shade. From the dentist to the patient, and finally to the dental technician, the entire process of the dental service team will be challenged when dealing with the hard-to-please patient when they are replacing an existing central crown.

The map of this passage looks like this:

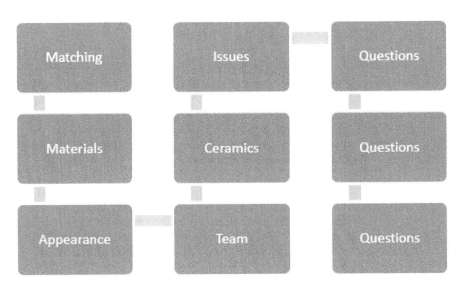

Questions:

1.

Which of the following is NOT a characteristic of a ceramic central?

A.
Zirconia

B.

Alumina

C.

PFM

D.

Yellow gold

E.

Presssable ceramics

2.

The adult human has _____ natural teeth.

A.

30

B.

32

C.

320

D.

31

E.

37

3.

One of the hardest things a dental technician can do is to:

A.

Make a crown in high-fusing porcelain

B.

To match a ceramic central

C.

To make a crown in low-fusing porcelain

D.

To take an accurate custom shade

E.

All of the above

4.

Which of the following contributes to patients having psychological issues regarding replacing a central porcelain crown:

A.

They suffered bullying during school

B.

They don't like going to the dentist

C.

They suffered trauma to their teeth at an early age

D.

Bad temporaries

E.

They come from an impoverished background

5.

The author states that it is difficult to match a central crown because:

A.

Patient's are attached to their old crowns

B.

Some patients have developed psychological issues regarding them

C.

Because of the wide selection of ceramic materials

D.

Because it is prominent and central to one's appearance

E.

All of the above

Answers:

1.
D
2.
B
3.
B
4.
C
5.
E

*DAT tip:* When I took the DAT the first essay was exactly the same one as the DAT booklet. It threw me; I thought it was a trick. The second essay was harder, and the third was the hardest. I was extra careful on the first and ran out of time on the last one. Be ready for the unexpected. Be sure to keep your focus.

# Quantitative Reasoning

**THE DAT MATH** section was harder than I thought. There was trigonometry and tricky algebra—half of the questions were word problems. I ran out of time and had to guess. The easy ones were no problem; the word problems were just that . . . a problem.

From what the test makers are saying, there will be less numerical calculations, conversions, geometry, and trigonometry and more questions on data analysis, interpretations and sufficiency, quantitative comparison; and probability and statistics.

All I can share is to develop good math techniques and to try to improve on your speed, work under time restrictions, and be prepared to work fast and with a good amount of word problems.

## Go for understanding, and then go for speed

There can be anything on the DAT, from math, algebra, geometry, and trigonometry. There are basic fractional calculations and word problems. Do the easy questions first, don't get hung up on the long difficult questions— leave those till the end.

**Possible concepts:**

- **Statistics**
- **Algebra**
- **Fractions**
- **Conversions: ounces, pounds, inches, feet**
- **Percentages**
- **Probability**
- **Geometry**
- **Trigonometry**
- **Word problems/applied math problems**
- **Rates**

**Units of measure**

**Length**

1 foot = 12 inches

1 yard = 3 feet

1 mile = 5280 feet

1 inch = 2.54 centimeters

1 centimeter = 10 millimeters

1 meter = 39.37 inches

**Weight**

1 pound = 16 ounces

1 ton = 2000 pounds

**Volume**

1 pint = 16 ounces

1 quart = 2 pints

1 gallon = 4 quarts

*DAT tip:* a note about the last part of the exam. Be sure to take the break they offer to give you a much needed mental break.

# BASIC MATH REVIEW

**MATH**: I never liked math, but developing my own speed math method made it interesting. I studied for probability and there was a question on that. There was a question on quadrants too.

You don't have to do math the way you were taught. The challenge has to do with speed. You might want to save the time-consuming questions for last. Make your own short cuts. The goal is to answer each question in under a minute. Push yourself to go faster.

Common short cuts:

Example: 1/8 = .125

Approximate the percentage of fractions:

Example:

1/2 = 50% = .50

1/4 = 25% = .25

1/6 = 16.67% = .1666

1/8 = 12.5% = .125

1/10 = 10% = .10

1/20 = 5% = .05

1/25 = 4% = .04

## Problems

1.
   Write 1/4 as a percent.
2.
   Write 1/5 as a percent.

## Solution

1.
   25%, .25
2.
   20%, .20

## Rate, base and percentage

Any math question can be asked and sometimes they include a percentage question.

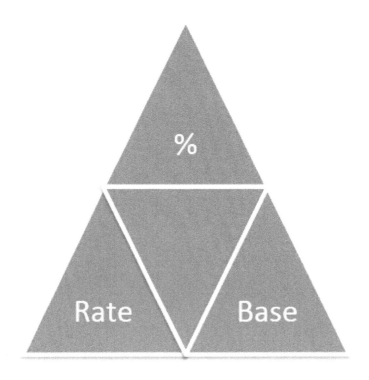

Percentage = Rate × Base

**Problems**

If 78% of the students in a physics class pass the course and there are 250 students in the class, how many students passed?

**Solution**

195

**Problem**

If 87% of the students pass the biology course and there are 50 students in the class, what is the amount of students that are expected to pass?

**Solution**

43.5

**Problem**

If you invest $10,000 for one year at 8.5 %, how much interest will you earn?

**Solution**

P = We are solving for P

R = the rate is 8 1/2 %

B = $10,000

R X B = P

.085 X $10,000 = $850

**Problem**

James sells a house at $10,000. If his commission rate is 5%, what is his commission?

**Solution**

Percentage = James commission

Rate = 5% or .05

Base = $10,000

P = R × B

.05 X $10,000 = $500

**Problem**

If Lance borrowed $4250 and was charged $417 in interest for one year, the interest rate would be:

    a)
        9%
    b)
        10%
    c)
        11%
    d)
        13%

e)

14%

**Solution**

The answer is B. 9.8%.

**Problem**

A salesman has a commission rate of 5.4%. If he wants to earn $2,000 in commissions, how much must he sell?

**Solution**

What is his base pay to make a commission?

$P = R \times B$

$B = P/R$

$B =$ is the unknown

$P = \$2,000$

$R = 5.4\%$ or .054

$B = \$2,000/.054 = \$37,037.04$

A check

$P = R \times B$

$\$37,037.04 \times 5.4\% = \$2,000$

**Problem**

What is the largest number?

   A.

      10/15

   B.

      14/18

   C.

      23/25

   D.

6/7

E.

7/8

## Solutions

Answer is C.

*DAT tip:* the test makers will try to trick you . . . the wrong answer will always be there. Sometimes you can work with the answer choices.

## TEST STRATEGIES

1.

Solve the easy ones first.

2.

Intelligent guessing . . . narrow it down to two answers.

3.

Blind guesses on answers (B).

Know your strengths and weaknesses, keep improving, and build up to test day. Keep practicing on problems.

# Perceptual Abilities Test

**MANUAL DEXTERITY** is important for the successful dentist, so it is crucial to score high in this area. When I took the exam it was both easier and harder than I thought. Some questions were simple, and others were crazy difficult.

The cube counting was okay, but got progressively harder. At the end there was an enormous block pattern that I hadn't seen before. I can't even guess how many blocks were on it, maybe fifty. So when you are preparing for the PAT be quick on what you know, and be prepared for some surprises. Again, as with the reading section I had extremely easy questions followed by very difficult ones. In my opinion, the test makers are trying to test your ability to keep disciplined and focused with easy questions followed by very hard ones. Don't let them throw you.

90 problems in 40 minutes:

What are they testing? These tests have proven to show perceptual abilities in dental school.

- Spacial

- Millimeter differences

- Two-dimensional to three-dimensional

## ANGLE RANKING

Take your time and develop your eyes to recognize larger and smaller angles. It takes practice. It has helped people to visualize the hands of a clock.

Visualize each angle as a right triangle. Most of these techniques are better if you devise your own method for accuracy and speed. It helps to experiment.

## CUBE COUNTING

Imagine if we painted these blocks (not including the bottoms). How many sides would be covered?

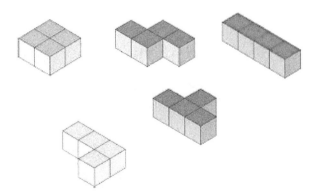

For those of you who want to get a jump on your competition there are many videos on YouTube that show the parts of the PAT. The key is to keep progressing and developing good techniques and speed.

Go to the DAT site to see what's on the exam. This was somewhat typical. One thing that helped me to visualize the cube counting was to stack children's blocks to replicate the designs of the cube formations.

I remember the PAT cube counting being harder than the practice tests that I took. There was a tower that would have made TRUMP proud.

## KEYHOLES

This is a situation where shapes are being pushed through a keyhole. Be careful, there is a tendency to make careless errors on here. This is a speed and accuracy test.

## HOLE PUNCHING

A paper is folded, and then a hole is punched in it. Always keep track of how many times you have folded the paper. The challenge is to predict what the paper will look like when you unfold it after it has been folded then punched.

*DAT tip:* this part was harder on the actual test. Try some actual hole punching to visualize how the paper unfolds.

## TOP/FRONT/END VIEWS

Compare the views and the lines. Do the lines match up? Sometimes the process of elimination works. This section probably takes longer than the cube counting. A dotted line means a change in the depth behind the plane, or a hidden feature.

## PATTERN FOLDING

You can make copies and cut out patterns and fold them into a box if that helps you to visualize. Imagine that you are folding the patterns over the possible answers.

*DAT tip:* the actual DAT was much harder than my preparation.

## KEEP SQUEEZING YOUR NOTES!

During your prep you will hear that you should be squeezing your notes. I think this is a good strategy and something you might consider doing. If the test preparation companies are saying it then it is probably a good idea to do it.

# Your Scores

**HOPEFULLY** you will have outstanding scores and will be celebrating after you take the DAT. Your scores will be given to you as:

**Academic average**

**Perceptual ability**

**Quantitative reasoning**

**Reading comprehension**

**Biology**

General chemistry

Organic chemistry

Total science

# Full-Length Exams

**IF I WAS** taking the DAT again, I would take an exam every day leading into test week. *Why?* It seemed like a test of endurance. After sitting for hours, with tired eyes and no caffeine, fatigue can set in which makes it difficult to concentrate. It takes commitment to perform well on test day.

# MENTAL VISUALIZATION

You should try to visualize taking the actual exam. From the clothes you'll be wearing, the dry erase board, the soundproof headphones (if you have them), the temperature in the room, and the people around you. This will be your mental marathon . . . build up to it.

*DAT tip:* treat the full-length exams like the real thing. Keep your scores, and make notes how you can improve.

# The Testing Center

**IT'S A GOOD IDEA** to go the test site one week early to get familiar with the drive. You might park, walk around the area, and possibly go inside to let them know that you are visiting one week ahead of your test date. You will be allowed to use an online calculator and a dry erase board. At the completion of your exam you will be given an unofficial score from the center. You can get the details at www.ada.org and at the Prometric website.

You probably want to visualize everything that you'll do that morning from brushing your teeth to what clothes you will wear. It helps to pre-plan your meal and to settle into a routine the week of the DAT. You might want to know the answers to these questions:

Will you be fingerprinted?

Will you be asked to empty out your pockets?

Will you be asked for two IDs with matching signatures?

Will they scan you for metal objects?

Will you have to pay for parking?

Will you have to place your jacket in a locker?

Will there be other DAT students taking their exams in the room with you?

Can you bring food, smoke or wear long earrings in the testing area?

Can you adjust the temperature of the room?

Can you wear a watch?

# MY EXAM DAY

I went to the test center one week ahead of time, parked my car, and walked to the testing site. On the day of the test, it helped that I had already been there. I already knew the environment from the scenery, the type of people and was familiar with the parking situation. As we impatiently waited for someone to open the door, I exchanged small talk with the person who would sit directly in front of me. He told me this was his second time taking the exam . . . that was info that I didn't really need to know.

I felt like I was prepared. I had attended Kaplan and went through the program twice. I studied hard and the day before the exam was able to relax and to not think about it. My last meal was spaghetti. On test day I was relaxed, confident, focused and ready.

SUCCESSFUL DAT STRATEGIES:

1.
   Go to the test site one week ahead. Park, locate the room, time the drive—was there a lot of traffic?

2.
   Eat a high-carb diet: lasagna, spaghetti, or meat and eggs.

3.
   Get plenty of rest the night before, but don't oversleep, just your regular routine.

4.
   Plan your fifteen minute break.

5.
   Dress in comfortable clothes.

6.

Bring juice, H2O, fruit, and snacks (raisins, granola bars, and carrots are good).

7.

Arrive at least one hour early.

8.

Bring Kleenex in case of the sniffles.

9.

Bring your documentations (2) with matching signatures.

10.

Research the way people are taking the exam by watching YouTube at the Prometric centers.

11.

Do something relaxing the day before.

12.

Have trouble sleeping? Try melatonin, sleepy time tea or watch a sleep video.

13.

Can you go five hours or longer without drinking coffee or smoking?

14.

Can you concentrate with noise reduction headphones?

15.

Match your biorhythms to the time you will be taking the DAT.

16.

Can you do a practice exam every day leading into exam day?

17.

Review your squeezed notes.

18.

Keep squeezing your notes.

# Rescheduling

**I'M SHARING THIS WITH YOU** to give you the heads-up on what can happen. These were the two weeks leading into the all-important DAT. Please take into consideration that I was a student living at home.

- 

My grandmother slept over for the weekend.

- 

I had to borrow money and it took the person one week to loan it to me. It felt like I was being held financially hostage. I wondered if I would have money for parking.

-

My uncle from Hawaii came over for a week.

•

Three days before the DAT, I was left to babysit my sick nephew and I caught a cold.

•

My car broke down during the week.

This was a lot of distractions. Be prepared for relatives to sneak up on you when you least expect it or when you least want to see them. At least my noisy neighbors didn't throw a loud party, which was customary for them on most weekends. I would say to prepare for the worst, and hope for the best. Looking back, I should have spent more time studying at the library. Rescheduling is a nice luxury to have—make use of it should you need it.

# Dental Exposure and Experience

**SHADOWING** or observing the work of the dentist is the most important thing you can do as a pre-dental student.

You may find a dentist who will help you in your dream to become a dentist. They are a helpful lot and most have made it by the kindness of others. Another way to get exposure in the field is to take pre-dental classes offered by dental schools.

Dental labs will sometimes help a future dental student or person looking into the dental industry. You can observe or even work part-time while learning lab procedures. For those who don't get in, it can be a good starting point into the dental lab industry.

Another way of getting exposure to dentistry is by taking dental lab classes at a community college. They offer classes like dental science, tooth anatomy and lab procedures.

# CHAPTER FIVE

# Application

*Behind every applicant is an interesting story*

**IF YOU'VE MADE IT** this far congratulate yourself. You have successfully navigated the pre-dental process. Approximately 41% gain acceptance at this point. Admissions will be looking at:

33% GPA

33% DAT

33% everything else

You can find information regarding application at www.ADEA.org.

*Application tip:* apply early! You will be more relaxed and there will be more empty seats when you apply. Once admission committees start filling seats the choosier they get. Remember to keep your application improving— your competition will be.

What are dental schools basing their acceptance on?

- Quality of your education
- General GPA

- Science GPA (including math)

- Units per semester

- DAT Scores

- Rating given by pre-dental advisors and professors

Everything else:

Awards, work experience, ability to finance school. Admissions are looking for evidence of consistently performing well academically and having extracurricular achievements.

What will be the criteria?

1.
   DAT scores, especially science
2.
   Course load, university and college attended
3.
   Academic background and your parent's education
4.
   Socioeconomic situation and barriers to achievement
5.
   Work experience and community and personal accomplishments
6.
   Location, letters, essay

The DAT is the all-important exam that compares applicants to each another. The GPA is in two sections: the science GPA and the general GPA. "Everything else" is the essay portion of the application, experience, letters of recommendation, ability to pay, and relevant dental experience. Most people say its 33% DAT, 33% GPA, and 33% everything else.

DAT breakdown of scores:

Academic average
Perceptual ability
Quantitative reasoning
Reading comprehension
Biology
General chemistry
Organic chemistry
Total science

Your science GPA:

Science and math GPA per semester.

General GPA:

Letters, essay, experience, parents and your background.

Boston University

One of the most important sources of information is the dental school's catalog. You have to choose the dental schools you apply to carefully. *Why?* Some schools don't accept out-of-state residents. Private schools usually accept the most out-of-state residents. Study the data . . . all you need is one school to accept you. You never know which school that might be. What if one school would have accepted you and you didn't apply to it?

*What's in your records?* Transcripts, letters of recommendation, and your photograph. What's the purpose to all this? Admissions are trying to select students who can complete the dental school program.

You may want to consult with your pre-dental advisor.
Select dental schools you want to apply to.

Current address
State or country
Zip code
Current telephone (where you can be reached)
Permanent address
City
State
Parental and family information
Parents' address
Zip code
Parents' telephone number
General information: indicate whether your parents are living or dead.
Parents' education: from elementary to graduate schools.

Parents' occupations
Number of brothers and sisters
Educational history: your high school
State
Year you graduated high school

Rank in class: high school. (i.e., if you were in the top 10% of your class, enter 1).

1.
    90 and over
2.
    75-89
3.
    50-74
4.
    25-49
5.
    1-24
6.
    Not Sure

They are wondering if you had any special accomplishments.

Undergraduate:

1.
    Freshman
2.

106

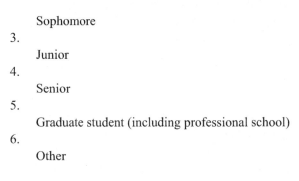

3.
Sophomore

4.
Junior

5.
Senior

6.
Graduate student (including professional school)

Other

Undergraduate major:

Undergraduate degree earned:

1.
A.A.

2.
B.A.

3.
B.S.

4.
Other

5.
None

Date of undergraduate degree

School conferring undergraduate degree
Dental certificate degree:

1.
R.D.H. (Registered Dental Hygienist)

2.
C.D.A. (Certified Dental Assistant)

3.
C.D.T. (Certified Dental Technician)

4.
Other

5.
None

The RDH is typically a four-year degree program with a board exam. The CDT is two written exams and a practical. The CDA is a series of exams.

Graduate major:

Graduate degree earned:

1.
M.A. (Master of Arts)
2.
M.S. (Master of Science)
3.
M.B.A. (Master of Business Administration)
4.
Other masters
5.
Ph.D.(Doctor of Philosophy)
6.
Other doctorate
7.
Other
8.
None

Date of graduate degree

School conferring graduate degree

Anticipated degree:

1.
A.A. (Associate of Arts)
2.
B.A. (Bachelor of Arts)
3.
B.S. (Bachelor of Science)
4.
M.A. (Master of Arts)
5.
M.S. (Master of Science)
6.
M.B.A. (Master of Business Administration)
7.
Ph.D. (Doctor of Philosophy)
8.
R.D.H. (Registered Dental Hygienist)

108

A.

    C.D.A. (Certified Dental Assistant)

B.

    C.D.T. (Certified Dental Technician)

C.

    Other

D.

    None

Anticipated                                                major
Date of anticipated degree/certificate

Degree/certification college code

Dental Admission Test: enter the month and year of the most recent time you took the DAT.

Academic average
Perceptual ability
Quantitative reasoning
Reading comprehension
Biology
General chemistry
Organic chemistry
Total science

Extracurricular activities: these items list various kinds of extracurricular activities you may have been involved in during your college or graduate school years. Enter one of the following numbers.

1.

    Participant

2.

    Participant and leader

Music
Athletics
Debate/Writing
Student Government
Health Services
Art/Drama
Sorority/Fraternity
Religious group
Community service
Political group

Other activity

*Application tip:* focus on a few things you are great at. Dental school admissions are looking for leaders, people who excel at what they love, not the person who is a participant in many things.

Personal data: enter the number of the month, day, and the last two digits of the year you were born.

City, state or county code where you were born
Country of citizenship
Sex
Ethnic identification:
Native American or Alaskan Native
Asian or Pacific Islander
Black or African-American
White or Caucasian (not of Hispanic origin)
Hispanic
Do not wish to report ethnic data
Not listed

Financial independence: do you consider yourself financially independent from your parents or guardian? Yes/No.
Percentage of expenses earned: What percentage of your undergraduate expenses (including tuition, books, and living expenses) did you earn? Enter the estimated percentage. For example, if you earned 50% please enter as 050. If you did not earn part of your undergraduate expenses, enter 000.

Finances expected:
Enter the estimated amount you expect to receive annually from each of the sources listed to finance your dental school education (including tuition, books, supplies, instruments and fees, but excluding living costs).

Financial independence

Percentage of earned finances
Parents/relatives
Savings/part-time work
Veterans' benefits
Other (grants, loans, etc.)
Number of dependents

**Supplementary information**: these items should be answered by 1 (yes) or 2 (no).

Typical questions:

Have you previously attended a health professional school?

Have you previously applied to but not attended a health professional school?

Will you apply to a health professional school (other than dental) this year?

Has your education ever been interrupted or affected adversely because of deficiencies in conduct or scholarship?

Has your education ever been interrupted or affected adversely for reasons other than conduct or scholarship?

Were you employed while attending college? If you had to work be sure to explain it here. They may see it as a reason for a lower GPA, or maybe your determination to becoming a dentist.

Did you hold summer jobs during your college years?

Do you have relatives who are dentists or are in dental school? As is expected it is beneficial if you have relatives that are professionals, especially dentists.

Are you currently in school?

Did you receive any scholastic honors in college?

Have you had any previous military experience?

May AADSAS release the information on this form to your pre-dental advisor?

Have you been contacted by the SELECT Dental Recruitment Program?

Has your dentist encouraged you to pursue a career in dentistry?

Complete course work entry: where you log in every class per semester/quarter followed by your grade and credit hours.

Personal data page:
*"Please state in concise terms what has motivated you toward a career in dentistry."*

Be honest in your application. It would be embarrassing to be caught in a lie during the interview.

# SELECTING SCHOOLS

Harvard University

**THE BEST SCHOOLS TO APPLY TO** are ones that you have the greatest chance for acceptance. Your list will probably include state schools where you are a resident, followed by private schools. You'll want to learn about their prerequisites, deadlines, what makes them unique and determine if they are a fit for you. Some schools are minority based; others may accept in-state resident students only. Do your due diligence, pick wisely, and be sure to pick enough of them.

I would like to say a word about out-of-state residents. This process is extremely competitive. It is not uncommon for admissions to select 15 out-of-state residents from a pool of 700. Therefore it is important to pick the schools where you have the best chance to get accepted.

**U.S. DENTAL SCHOOLS**

Alabama

❏
    University of Alabama School of Dentistry, Birmingham

Arizona

❏
    A.T. Still University, Arizona School of Dentistry and Oral
    Health, Mesa

❏
    Midwestern University College of Dental Medicine Arizona,
    Glendale

California

❏
    Loma Linda University School of Dentistry, Loma Linda

❏
    University of California, Los Angeles School of Dentistry, Los
    Angeles

❏
    University of California, San Francisco School of Dentistry, San
    Francisco

❏
    University of the Pacific Arthur A. Dugoni School of Dentistry,
    San Francisco

❏
    The Herman Ostrow School of Dentistry of USC, Los Angeles

❏
    Western University of Health Sciences College of Dental
    Medicine, Pomona

Colorado

❏
    University of Colorado School of Dental Medicine, Aurora

113

University of Connecticut

Connecticut

☐
   University of Connecticut School of Dental Medicine,
   Farmington

District of Columbia

☐
   Howard University College of Dentistry, Washington

Florida

☐
   Lake Erie College of Osteopathic Medicine School of Dental
   Medicine, Bradenton

☐
   Nova Southeastern University College of Dental Medicine, Fort
   Lauderdale

☐
   University of Florida College of Dentistry, Gainesville

Georgia

☐
   Georgia Regents University College of Dental Medicine,
   Augusta

Illinois

☐

114

Midwestern University College of Dental Medicine, Downers Grove

☐

University of Illinois at Chicago College of Dentistry, Chicago

☐

Southern Illinois University School of Dental Medicine, Alton

Indiana

☐

Indiana University School of Dentistry, Indianapolis

Iowa

☐

University of Iowa College of Dentistry, Iowa City

Kentucky

☐

University of Kentucky College of Dentistry, Lexington

☐

University of Louisville School of Dentistry, Louisville

Louisiana

☐

Louisiana State University School of Dentistry, New Orleans

Maine

☐

University of New England College of Dental Medicine, Portland

Maryland

☐

University of Maryland at Baltimore School of Dentistry, Baltimore

Tufts Dental School

Massachusetts

☐

Boston University Henry M. Goldman School of Dental Medicine, Boston

☐

Harvard School of Dental Medicine, Boston

☐

Tufts University School of Dental Medicine, Boston

Michigan

☐

University of Michigan School of Dentistry, Ann Arbor

☐

The University of Detroit Mercy School of Dentistry, Detroit

Minnesota

☐

University of Minnesota School of Dentistry, Minneapolis

Mississippi

☐

University of Mississippi Medical Center of Dentistry, Jackson

Missouri

116

☐

University of Missouri-Kansas City School of Dentistry, Kansas City

☐

Missouri School of Dentistry: Oral Health at A.T. Still University, Kirksville

Nebraska

☐

University of Nebraska Medical Center College of Dentistry, Lincoln

☐

Creighton University School of Dentistry, Omaha

Nevada

☐

University of Nevada at Las Vegas School of Dental Medicine, Las Vegas

New Jersey

☐

Rutgers School of Dental Medicine, Newark

New York

☐

Columbia University College of Dental Medicine, New York City

☐

New York University College of Dentistry, New York City

☐

State University of New York at Buffalo School of Dental Medicine, Buffalo

☐

State University of New York at Stony Brook School of Dental Medicine, Stony Brook

North Carolina

117

□ University of North Carolina School of Dentistry, Chapel Hill

□ East Carolina University School of Dental Medicine, Greenville

Ohio

□ The Ohio State University College of Dentistry, Columbus

□ Case Western Reserve University School of Dental Medicine, Cleveland

Oklahoma

□ University of Oklahoma College of Dentistry, Oklahoma City

Oregon

□ Oregon Health and Science University School of Dentistry, Portland

University of Pittsburgh

Pennsylvania

□

Temple University, Maurice H. Komberg School of Dentistry, Philadelphia

☐

University of Pennsylvania School of Dental Medicine, Philadelphia

☐

University of Pittsburgh School of Dental Medicine, Pittsburgh

## Puerto Rico

☐

University of Puerto Rico School of Dentistry, San Juan

## South Carolina

☐

Medical University of South Carolina College of Dental Medicine, Charleston

## Tennessee

☐

University of Tennessee Health Sciences Center College of Dentistry, Memphis

☐

Meharry Medical College School of Dentistry, Nashville

## Texas

☐

Texas A&M Health Sciences Center, Baylor College of Dentistry, Dallas

☐

University of Texas Health Science Center at Houston School of Dentistry, Houston

☐

The Dental School at the University of Texas Health Science Center at San Antonio, San Antonio

## Utah

☐

University of Utah College of Dentistry, Salt Lake City

☐

Rosemen University of Health Sciences College of Dental Medicine, South Jordan

Virginia

☐

Virginia Commonwealth University School of Dentistry, Richmond

Washington

☐

University of Washington School of Dentistry, Seattle

West Virginia

☐

West Virginia University School of Dentistry, Morgantown

Wisconsin

☐

Marquette University School of Dentistry, Milwaukee

**Schools with a high percentage of out-of-state students**

Meharry: 90% (this is a predominantly African-American school)

University of Pennsylvania: 82% (some schools have special acceptance deals with neighboring states)

Case School of Dental Medicine: 74%

New York University: 74%

University of Pittsburgh: 55%

Temple: 52%

Marquette: 50% (check to see if your state residency is favorable)

Virginia Commonwealth: 40%

From the ADEA.org site.

**New schools**

1997 Nova Southeastern

2002 University of Nevada Las Vegas

2003 A.T. Still University

2007 Midwestern University

2009 Western University (Pomona)

2011 East Carolina University

2011 Roseman University

2011 Midwestern University

2012 Lake Erie College of Osteopathic Medicine

**Dental school closures**

1986 Oral Roberts University

1988 Emory University

1990 Georgetown University

1990 Fairleigh Dickenson

1991 Washington University (Saint Louis)

1993 Loyola University

2001 Northwestern

2013 University of New England

2013 A.T. Still University

2013 University of Utah

2015 Bluefield College

What is the best school for you? The one that will let you in. I had a friend that went through the process and was accepted by one school. That's all he needed—he is a practicing dentist today.

University of Michigan

# Essay

*Please state in concise terms why you are interested in the dental profession. Include any additional information: extracurricular activities, extra degrees, experience, research, publications, etc.*

Your personal statement isn't creative writing. This is not the place to write your novel, nor is it a marketing exercise. This is your life, what motivated you to become a dentist, and hopefully a compelling story that pulls everything together for the admissions committee.

What to write:

- Your story and why are you interested in the profession
- Is there anything that makes you unique?
- Extracurricular activities
- Secondary majors or degrees
- Experience in a healthcare delivery setting
-

122

- Pertinent research

- Publications, etc.

- Personal feelings

- Professional interests

- Achievements

- Good grammar

What not to write:

- Don't lie

- Don't show off

- Don't criticize the profession

Check out the Student Network Doctor site to see what essays worked and those that didn't. Remember to tell a story, to be unique and to be interesting. You have several options, from writing it yourself to hiring a freelance writer.

Writing process:

1. Organize your thoughts, write a rough draft and let it sit for awhile.

2. Start with a strong opening sentence.

3. End the paragraphs so the reader wants to keep reading.

4. Develop key points to keep your writing moving along; organize each paragraph.

5. Keep the reader in mind. Does it tie your application together or offer anything new about you?

Examples:

The event that made you interested in dentistry.

How it changed your life.

The time you overcame an obstacle—your lowest point.

Your conflict—and application.

How you are different than before—and grew in the process.

Write about yourself as a remarkable character in your story, but this is not creative writing. This is your personal story, not a flowery chance to show how many words you can fit on a piece of paper. Tell a story about how you became interested in becoming a dentist, with supporting facts so the admissions committee feels like they have everything they need to know. Hopefully this will lead to you getting invited for an interview.

Be entertaining and let them get to know you; write in a personable, friendly, warm and professional manner. "Show rather than tell" in your descriptions.

Be humble, but tell them about yourself. Be honest—you wouldn't want them to catch you in a lie. Know that some of your classmates may exaggerate their accomplishments. Sometimes they get caught in a lie, sometimes they don't.

ADDRESS YOUR AUDIENCE

Write to your audience, in this case it's the admissions committee. What are they looking for? Admitting students who can survive the academic program and to add value to their classes and school. Keep it simple; address the reader; tell your thoughts and feelings. Tell a great story.

PAST, PRESENT, FUTURE

Why dentistry? What are your future goals and why? Who are the important, influential people in your life and why? Tie it together.

Give a big problem and how you overcame it. This is the same technique writers use to create depth with characters. Give your main character a big problem.

UNIQUENESS

What makes you unique? Any special situations not included in your application to this point? Stand out in a good way, not in a way that will give them pause for concern. Make it exciting.

124

## EXPOSURE

Be a leader! Use social media to support your cause. Will admissions Google you? Who knows? It couldn't hurt to manage what they see. Starting a dental blog or creating a YouTube channel on dentistry, writing on forums, and guest blogging are all things that can help bring awareness to you.

## PASSION FOR DENTISTRY

This is your chance to sell yourself and to answer that big question—"So why do you want to be a dentist?" If you are truly passionate about dentistry it will show in your essay.

## IS YOUR LIFE CONSISTENT WITH YOUR BRAND?

Are you honest, responsible, hard-working, disciplined, or someone looking for shortcuts. What about the cultural, social, and family aspects of your life? Does your economic situation help or hurt your chances? It can help to talk to other dental students or pre-dental students about your essay.

## ARE YOU COMPETITIVE?

Do you play sports? Have you won awards? Are you a winner? They are looking for a leader in a few things that you are passionate about. When you set your mind on something are you an outstanding achiever?

## LEADERSHIP

What are those few things you've done in your life that are great? Will you give the admissions committee confidence that you have the determination to complete a goal like dental school? Any examples of you doing this?

## PROOFREADING

Are you interested in making your application shine? Have you considered hiring an editor to proofread your writing? Proofreading will give your writing a professional touch. With so much riding on your application can you afford not to have someone proofread your essay?

Terms to know:

*Proofreading:* you submit your work to them, then they send a proofread copy back to you. You can make corrections from that file.

*Editing:* an editor will research, proofread, give you input on sentence structure, etc. Some people charge by the word and it can be very expensive. Probably too expensive for the typical pre-dental student.

*Freelance writer:* they will write your essay after you give them an outline of your strong points you want mentioned. Some of these writers may even be dentists, hygienists, and dental students themselves.

# Letters

**YOUR LETTERS** of recommendation should come from your advisor or the person in charge of the pre-dental department. You want to select the highest-ranking person who will give you the best recommendation. Professors can be a good choice. You should find out if your school keeps a file on each student. If they do you should ask professors if they will send a letter of recommendation to the admissions office.

Don't let years pass before you ask for a positive letter as they might forget you. Your best letter writers will be in classes you recently completed and did well in. Speaking up in class and contributing in discussions takes courage, but it can help in the learning that takes place between instructors and students. Help your teacher and they most likely will appreciate and remember you. One thing is talking to an empty space of pre-meds, the other is a stimulating conversation.

While advisors and professors are solid choices, pastors, employers, and friends are not. You should go with the people who knew you in the academic setting as this is what dental school is. You might want to remind your academic friends that you are:

- Intelligent
- Ambitious
- Virtuous
- Honest

This is a time when you want to keep your friends close in case you need positive character references.

# Interview

**WHO WILL BE** interviewing you? Anyone from the director of admissions, a member of the admissions committee, a student advisor, whoever it is—they will be asking questions and will be evaluating you. This is the time to put your best foot forward.

Try to create a good impression. Help the interviewer to fill in the gaps in your application and to link each phase of your life. You will be evaluated on your appearance, personality, maturity and communication skills. Your dress should be classic, solids, suit jacket, or formal with a professional manner.

*Tell me about yourself:* This is your sales pitch. Preferably, you will be able to mention things that are not on your application and personal statement. This is not the time to be controversial; honesty and integrity are the way to go.

*Why do you want to be a dentist?* This one question tells a lot about you. You have to be honest with yourself as well as the interviewer. Is it for the money? Are your parents dentists? Do you like working with your hands? Do you want to own a practice, are you fascinated with the field, or maybe you were inspired by your dentist? This is the question that allows you to tell your story. Remember that they may be referring to the personal statement section on your application.

Be prepared to talk about financing. I had gone to a financial aid seminar that helped explain the details on financing dental school. The only thing that I can share is to apply early and that some schools may perform a credit check. You might want to contact each school if you have concerns in this area.

**Things to do:**

Maintain comfortable eye contact.

Have a professional handshake, a slight squeeze, a nod and eye contact to bond with your interviewer.

Have a conforming, comfortable, and conservative appearance.

Be personable to get know your interviewer.

Present a pleasant appearance; it's not a time to showcase your individuality.

Don't cross your legs.

Be aware of your expressions, from your frown and body language to your smile.

Arrive 30-90 minutes early.

Send a short thank you note ten days after.

Possible questions you might be asked:

Where do you see yourself ten years from now?

Why our dental school?

What courses did you like or dislike the most?

What experience has been the most valuable to you?

What did you like about shadowing a dentist?

Do you have any relatives or friends in dentistry?

What are the hobbies you excel at?

Do you like working with your hands?

What are your favorite books and magazines to read?

Did you work?

Discuss your DAT scores.

What will you do if you are rejected?

Have you given thought to what you would do if you don't get in? Any backup plans or thoughts of reapplying? Would you be willing to raise your GPA or go on to graduate school?

At the end of your interview you will be asked if you have any questions. You should have 3-5 questions to ask them. Bring a notebook if that helps you. Research the school to find out what makes it unique and note any questions you might have.

**Things NOT to do:**

Don't use it as a time to show off your two-month-old beard.

Don't use it as a chance to show the latest chest bump you learned at spring break.

Don't cross your legs. You will appear aloof, self-assured, cocky.

Don't flirt or ask your interviewer out on a date. Winking is not recommended. Avoid excessive touching at all costs.

Don't pass gas no matter how bad the urge. If it does happen, use it as an opportunity to explain your knowledge of the digestive system.

This is probably not the place to voice your opinions on how you would overhaul the healthcare system.

Please refer to Asdanet.org for more questions and advice. There are several books that go in depth on the personal interview section of dental school.

## What Are They Looking For?

**WHAT** are the admissions committees looking for when they make up their dental school class? They are looking for students who can complete the program. They will consider your:

- Quality of education

- GPA

- Number of poor grades

- Number of classes that were dropped

-

- Number of units taken per semester

- DAT scores

- Pre-dental advisors

- Extracurricular activities

- Work experience

- A great personal story on your essay

- Source(s) of financing for college

The most important being:

Overall and science GPA; DAT reading; pre-dental advisor; years in school; PAT; pattern of GPA; and your DAT science scores will have to match your science GPA.

From what I observed the successful candidates also exhibited a high tolerance to pain, a positive attitude, a sense of humor, the ability to bond with classmates, a respect to teachers and others and the ability to get along with people.

*Imagine if you were put in charge of bringing together a dental school class. You would want a dynamic mix of people with great potential who would push each other to greater levels of achievement. You would want them to be able to get along, have some people who will publish scientific articles, and each one a spokesman of the learning that occurred in your graduating class. The worst-case scenario would be if people were to drop out without the means to pay for their student loans.*

# Calendar Year

**APPLYING TO DENTAL SCHOOL** is a lengthy process that takes over a year and takes careful planning. Please check with individual school catalogues, the ADEA official guide, your school and your advisor.

Keep in mind there are deadlines to consider in each of these important areas:

☐
Register and take the DAT

☐

Organize the letters of recommendation

☐

Application

☐

Secondary application

☐

Interviews

# Dental School

**GETTING IN** dental school is not easy; completing it is even more difficult. First-year students are introduced to a world where their time is spent attending classes, studying and preparing for exams, all while juggling a huge course load.

*One of my friends made it to dental school and told me he was upset at me . . . he said, "I thought I was going to die."*

These are the types of classes that are required for first- and second-year dental students:
Anatomy
Anesthesia
Bacteriology
Biochemistry
Dental materials
Endodontics
Histology
Pathology
Pharmacology
Physiology

Plus dental-related classes from diagnosis and oral anatomy to prosthodontics.

The first and second year involves pre-clinical and brings sleepless nights studying, followed by the boards. The third and fourth years are mostly spent doing the clinical work of a dentist and are followed by the clinical boards. Some schools require freshmen dental students to have a collection of extracted teeth. Contact the dental schools to find out if this applies to you.

# Financial Aid

**FINANCIAL ASSISTANCE** programs come in federal, state, military, school, and other aid programs. There are scholarships from private foundations, religious organizations to working in underserved communities. Most students receive some sort of financial aid. You will be asked for a detailed history of your assets and cash flows. How you will pay for dental school is an important decision and some dental schools offer financial aid seminars.

## Live like a student

If you are lucky your parents started investing for your education when you were born. There are several investments to choose from. If you are a parent wanting to set up an education account your CFP (certified financial planner) should be consulted.

Did you know that you may qualify to get free federal money? It's true for the most part, but whatever assets you have you are expected to use first before you can receive grants. The government expects you to use all your assets (including investments in a business) for your education before they will give you any grant money.

As an undergraduate I had business property and had to sell the equipment before I could receive a financial aid package that included grants and loans. Grants do not have to be paid back and they give the student an option of not having to work at a job.

My biggest mistake was buying a Mazda RX7 while I was a pre-dental student. This forced me to work more hours than I was already working. It ended up on my credit cards. You definitely want to avoid charging on your cards and having to deal with additional financial stress.

## You are not a doctor yet!

After you announce your plans that you want to become a dentist you will have new opportunities that will come your way. Some will be in the romantic department, others in leadership opportunities. The problem is they all cost time and money and you may not be able to work for years.

*Pre-dental tip:* since dental school is expensive, the financial status of a student is carefully considered.

# Your Money

**APPLYING TO DENTAL SCHOOL** is expensive. You definitely want to save up for your DAT and application expenses. From the DAT preparation study guides, pre-dental classes and books, the journey to become a dentist is a big investment. I was raising money to pay for classes, DAT prep, car payments, insurance, credit cards, and the application. At the end I didn't make it and had to postpone my application to the following year. By failing to plan, I had to apply a year later—it's a year of my life that I'll never get back.

*Pre-dental tip:* some of the prime spots for work/study are given to future doctors. Let them know if you are available or interested.

## Delayed gratification

Dental school is similar to financing a house. Be the person a banker would loan money to.

As an undergrad you might feel that you need a sports car (after all your classmates have them) or that new suit or dress, maybe a dog to keep you company. After all you are a "future" doctor. It might be a good thing to postpone that purchase until you have completed dental school. Why? You have some expenses coming up on the horizon.

Tuition and books

DAT preparation materials

Time off from work to prepare for the DAT

Living expenses

Paying to take the DAT

Application fee

Travel to interviews

Clothes for the interview

If you are receiving financial aid you shouldn't plan on taking too much time off from school.

*Pre-dental tips:* take pride in your ability to stretch a dollar—it is far better to be frugal than to spend money unwisely before you are a dentist.

# Your Credit

**MY CREDIT WAS BAD,** yet I qualified for student aid. I'm sure that I was not a preferred borrower and the pre-dental road was harder. If you fall in this group you might want to contact the financial aid department of the dental schools at which you plan to apply. Some of the health profession loans require a credit check while others do not.

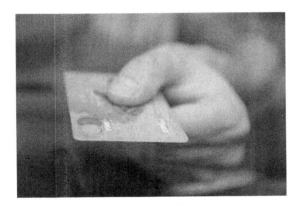

Debt

If I could share one thing to help students it would be to apply to the financial aid office as soon as possible. I waited and found out later that I could receive grants and loans, but one of my biggest mistakes was to charge too many things on my credit cards. Having excessive debt on credit cards forced me to work more hours that I should have.

# LOANS

Lending institutions may require a credit check for some student loans. From what I remember the guaranteed student loans from the government didn't require a credit check. Most students get their financing through the federal government. There are alternative loan programs. If you are in this group you have to do your homework.

By agreeing to work in a dentist-deprived area, some underrepresented places in the U.S. will pay/support dental students for a year in return for them to practice in their cities for a year after graduation.

It's your responsibility to finance (and pay off) your dental school education. Remember the student loan is a loan that needs to be repaid. These loans must be paid off, even after death.

# CHAPTER SIX

# Minority &Disadvantaged Students

**AS A MINORITY AND DISADVANTAGED STUDENT** I understand the additional challenges facing the student from an economically challenged background. I became part of the disadvantaged group by way of my parents' divorce when I was thirteen. There is more stress, less support, a harder time paying for college, critical relatives and fewer role models. The data shows that growing up in a fatherless or divorced home contributes to poverty. If you find yourself as part of the disadvantaged group, you will have additional challenges beyond studying. Admissions committees refer to this as "barriers to achievement."

Percentage of fatherless children that are poor: 37.1%

Percentage of married two-parent family's children that are poor: 6.8%

(U.S. Census 2007-2009 data/heritage.org)

Minority applicants make up to 13% of the applicant pool. This includes African-Americans, Latinos, Native Americans, Native Alaskans, Hawaiians, and other Pacific Islanders. African-Americans have a higher percentage dropout rate than non-blacks.

What admissions considers:

- 
  Your academic background
- 
  Your parents' education
-

## Socioeconomic situation and barriers to achievement

Why is the socioeconomic situation so important? For one, dental school is expensive. For two, poor students have a higher dropout rate and are more likely to default on their student loans.

In a study by *Forsyth and Furlong* they examined the socioeconomic disadvantaged and followed their experiences in graduate school—they found that certain factors affect the disadvantaged including:

- Fear of debt

- Lack of confidence and role models

- Cultural isolation

A fear of debt forces disadvantaged students to work more hours, usually at low-wage jobs not associated with their field of study. Working while their classmates are busy studying, joining clubs, networking with college alumni, and volunteering in scientific research puts the student at a disadvantage.

A lack of confidence makes "poor" students quit sooner than their classmates. Add the lack of social networking that minorities and the poor face and it's a tough hole to rise out of. Another issue is the family's isolation that may exist when one member tries to break out of familiar norms for the group.

Cultural, social, and family isolation is another drawback the disadvantaged suffer from compared to the children of the wealthy. Wealthy parents have the ability to help financially, culturally, socially, and usually have fewer children. Their family's makeup tends to support their children's ambitious dreams. The families of minority and socio-disadvantaged students suffer from a lack of role models and confidence, their skeptical family members often pile on the feelings of self-doubt while their educational debt is rising and job opportunities seem to be diminishing.

# FATHERLESS

There is one group of people who will have more challenges than anyone. Unfortunately they make up a large percentage of the population. These are the "fatherless" kids of divorced or never-married parents. Basically children of "fatherless" households have a harder time with poverty, behavioral problems, overly cautious males, and teenage girls having children with a high rate of divorce. I believe this is what admissions calls "barriers to achievement."

Fatherless children are presented with more obstacles than children that were raised in a two-parent household. One of the main things is learning how to manage money. Financing school, learning to avoid credit cards, living within a budget, not working excessively, living with student loan debt— these are things that disadvantaged students struggle with.

Critical families that marginalize the ambitious student's goals compound the lack of confidence they already have. Students often worry if they will be able to find a job after graduation. They are fighting their self-doubts, concerns about the future and their family when they announce they want to become a dentist.

MALES:

*When I sought help from my dad for help he asked, "Who do you think you are?" Our parents are not proper role models for this kind of goal.*

80% of rapists motivated with displaced anger come from fatherless homes (Criminal Justice and Behavior, Vol 14)

70% of juveniles in state-operated institutions come from fatherless homes (Source: U.S. Dept. of Justice, Special Report)

85% of all youths sitting in prisons grew up in a fatherless home (Source: Fulton County Georgia jail populations, Texas Dept. of Corrections 1992)

Children from fatherless homes are:

•

- 32 times more likely to run away

- 20 times more likely to have a behavioral disorder

- 20 times more likely to end up in prison

- 14 times more likely to commit rape

- 10 times more likely to abuse chemical substances

- 9 times more likely to drop out of high school

- 5 times more likely to be poor

- 5 times more likely to commit suicide

Information from the Center for Children's Justice

FEMALES:

Not to be outdone, fatherless females have their own challenges:

71% of high school female dropouts come from fatherless homes (National Principals Association report)

75% of adolescent female patients in chemical abuse centers come from fatherless homes

164% are more likely to have a premarital birth

92% of fatherless females are likely to have a divorce (U.S. Dept. of Health and Human Services)

If you grew up in a fatherless household you will have more challenges than the traditional student.

# BARRIERS TO ACHIEVEMENT?

What is it?

- Lack of finances

-

Fear of educational debt

- Low expectations

- Cultural, societal, and family isolation: maybe you are the first person in your family to go to graduate school?

Status: a measure of an individual's or family's economic and social position in relation to others based on income, education, occupation and residence.

We know the odds are stacked against the poor and favor the wealthy. That's reality. Wealthy parents can educate their children in private schools from elementary to high school. They have more resources. Their educational investment yields a better return from attending prep school, private school, having tutors and better teachers, alumni, a beautiful campus, wealthy classmates, and safety, among other things. They are generally more confident, have more financial support, and have a richer cultural heritage.

If you are the first person in your family to go to college or to apply for professional school, you should know that your path won't be easy, from having to work, suffering critical relatives, attending low-performance schools, and having an overall slower path to success. You are going to have to be stronger than the average pre-dental student.

Nothing is impossible, the word itself says 'I'm Possible'

Ten things to consider

1.

Don't use those credit cards!

2.

Embrace frugality.

3.

Live a doctor's lifestyle AFTER you become one.

4.

Announce that you are pre-dental later in the process; this will allow you to test your abilities without the critical voices of relatives.

5.

Take up a hobby to gain self-confidence and to raise your GPA.

6.

Take up guitar, golf, piano, and improve on your study skills.

7.

Teach something.

8.

Find a mentor or role model.

9.

Make it a practice to visit museums and concerts to gain cultural awareness.

10.

Think positive (GROW as a person).

11.

Apply for financial aid early!

12.

Become the one who overcomes obstacles.

Some examples of successful people who grew up fatherless:

George Washington, Thomas Jefferson, Bill Clinton, Barack Obama, Nelson Mandela, Jackie Robinson, Oprah Winfrey, John Lennon, J.R.R. Tolkien, Sir Isaac Newton, Leonardo da Vinci, Johann Sebastian Bach, Linus Pauling, Irving Berlin, and Dr. Ben Carson.

*Does like beget like?* In some cases it does, but are you that special applicant that they are looking for? The person who has overcome adversity his or her whole life?

# Family & Friends

Kihei, Maui

**MOM'S LIFE BEGAN** in Maui, Hawaii. She was just two years old when the Japanese Zeros flew overhead on their way to Pearl Harbor, my grandmother cheering them on, not knowing their mission. My grandmother grew up in Japan, my grandfather on Maui. Grandpa must have felt surrounded—his parents and his new wife were from Fukushima. Like many of the Japanese in Hawaii he had a Japanese face, but was raised an American. My grandparents' legacy was born of the fights they had and how she sought shelter in the homes of caring neighbors and the sugarcane fields. People called my grandfather Mike . . . as American as you get.

Mom went to school barefooted. They had no TV, just the radio, and she remembers how my grandfather would listen to baseball games on the radio.

He remained a lifelong baseball fan throughout his life and we shared the same love for the game.

Much has been said about my grandfather, how he fought with the police and landed in jail, how he terrorized my grandmother, mom and her siblings and fought with everyone around him. How he drank and chased his family away into the cold dark of night, with them scared for their lives, hiding in the long wisps of the graceful sugarcane. I can only go from what I know. I was his spoiled grandson whom he cherished—he was my refuge from my father's beatings.

During World War Two the Japanese who lived in Hawaii were not put into concentration camps like on the mainland, but coincidently they lived in what were called camps—mom was in Camp Two. They provided plantation owners the labor to harvest the sugarcane and pineapple that grew plentiful in Hawaii's tropical climate. Gramps was an electrician on the plantation, grams did whatever work she could find—mostly her work was cleaning the plantation owners' homes. Yes, my grams was a maid; she was also my strongest supporter and friend.

## Barriers to achievement?

In a first of its kind study of socioeconomically disadvantaged graduate students, the authors *Forsyth and Furlong* followed a group of such disadvantaged students through higher education and found that "poor" students had issues that other students didn't have. These barriers to achievement included a loss of confidence, a fear of debt, a lack of proper role models, and concerns about finding work after graduation.

I included the following story to show what the background of a socioeconomic disadvantaged student looks like. The barriers to achievement may be anything from a parent's drinking problem, to a parental divorce or loss of job, to growing up in a war-torn country. If any of this applies to you, be aware it is taken into consideration as "barriers to achievement."

While I went to school I lived with my mom, my recently divorced and chemically addicted younger sister, and her seven-year-old son. Life there was chaos. My shift at the dental lab was 5 pm to midnight. After work I would take a quick shower, eat, and then study until I fell asleep. Then classes began at 9 am. During those days I rarely had enough time to study, prepare lab reports and routinely crammed for exams.

*Pre-dental tip:* it is not advisable to cram for chemistry, biology and physics as these subjects are based upon prior knowledge. You will fall further behind.

Five people you might meet in your family:

*The Mom*: beware of the "damsel in distress" syndrome. Let's face it, there are some of us who are raised by mothers who crave sympathy and attention. The single mother has a lot on her plate. She didn't plan on raising a family on her own. Unfortunately this weak leadership will cause chaos in the house. If this is where you study, there's going to be trouble.

*The uncle:* my family had an intervention where my uncle told me, "I wasn't smart enough to become a doctor." *Hmm, I thought "how did he know how smart I was?"* Growing up in a dysfunctional home was difficult and not good for this goal, but when you don't have the money your options are limited.

"You aren't smart enough"

*The sibling rivalry:* my sister would leave her seven-year-old son with me while I prepared for the DAT. She would leave at night, sometimes would return later the next day, then would sleep until evening. At night she would disappear once again and we would repeat the drama. How could I study like this? I'll never forget the look of relief on her face when I told her I didn't get into dental school.

*The nephew:* my family pitted me against a seven-year-old. My "job" was to mentor him because he mentioned once that he wanted to become a medical doctor. A few weeks before my DAT, I finally reached my breaking point and stopped talking to him. So mom called my pastor, my friend who was in law school, and another friend who was a pre-dent the week before my DAT. They called to see why mom was bothering them. It was a distraction; I had to apologize.

*The dad:* I rarely spoke to dad during my pre-dental years. With my credit cards maxed out, he was my last resort. I asked him if I could borrow money for DAT prep. He never called me back. I had to postpone my application for one year.

Welcome to the world of the *socio-disadvantaged student with barriers to achievement* as a pre-dental student. It becomes glaringly clear why admissions labels these types of students. This is what some of us must endure as we go through the process of applying to dental school.

## REJECTION

## Plan B

IT'S SOMETHING WE don't want to think about, but it does happen. Many students who start off as pre-meds and pre-dents won't make it. To not get in at this point is beyond disappointing. I missed weddings and funerals. Why? This goal takes sacrifice. It's that hard folks. I was one of the many that didn't make it to dental school.

# You may have failed, but you are not a failure!

I will tell you what your advisors probably won't tell you. From the start of your goal from general chemistry to graduating dental school, the success rate is approximately 10%. One out of ten will become a dentist. These are very smart, capable students.

There are approximately 100,000 dentists in the United States—every year approximately 12,000 students apply to dental school and 5,000 are accepted.

Let's take a hypothetical class of 1,000 new pre-dental majors. They enroll and take one year of biology, general chemistry, and physics and by the end of organic chemistry there are roughly 200 left.

Those 200 apply to dental school.

Of those, 82 (or 41%) are accepted into dental school.

Then, 1% to 10% may drop out of dental school (with minorities having a higher dropout rate).

Which leaves approximately 80 students from our pool of 1,000, or 8%. Of the 118 rejected applicants some will reapply and will gain admission on the second try.

## I made it to the hospital

I was sitting on the examining table, no longer a future dentist, but wondering if I would make it out alive—I was the victim of a bout of depression that led to pneumonia. As I slowly made my way to the entrance of the hospital, people scurried around me. When I was healthy I walked with a sense of purpose—now I was an obstacle who slowed them down. I had no money and had to rely on mom's generosity to pay for the meds that would keep me alive. I could barely breathe; the disappointment of not getting into dental school sapped my energy as I coughed up a thick green mucus that dangerously filled my lungs. By the time I reached the office I was out of breath and had serious concerns I was going to die.

I wished that I had a better understanding of how I would feel if I didn't get into dental school. The book that helped me the most was Nancy K. Schlossberg and Susan Porter Robinson's *GOING TO PLAN B: How You Can Cope, Regroup, and Start Your Life on a New Path*. Have you wondered what you will do if you don't get in?

## Not everyone gets in, failure is a possibility

When I got my rejection notices I felt like a failure. All that hard work for nothing—it seemed like such a huge waste of time and money. If I was to do it over I would have taken a vacation, or maybe a change in school would have been better. A new environment would help in terms of starting with a clean slate.

It's a challenge to put your life in order, but now you have an important decision to make. *Should you reapply or quit?* It's a good idea to consult with your advisor on this important decision.

Options:

- Improve your application and reapply with a higher DAT; more significant experience; a higher science GPA; and a higher overall GPA.

- Apply to graduate school or another professional school.

- Change your major.

Many successful dentists applied more than once, took classes more than once, and even failed the board exams. Probably the one thing that will help you most is to maintain a positive attitude.

## If you don't get in will you reapply?

# AUTOPSY OF A FAILURE

Probably the best thing you can do is to contact the school and ask *why* you were rejected and what things you can do to improve your application. Perhaps admissions wants you to mature a bit, or to improve your science GPA. It might be a good idea to ask them.

Remember that they didn't reject you, but your application—and you can improve that. Even the great investor Warren Buffett was rejected when he applied to Harvard for his MBA. (He was accepted to Columbia and is considered one of the best investors of all time).

Access your skills; this is not something you want to do if math and science are your weaknesses. News alert: pre-meds and your classmates are ambitious, and math and science are their strong suits. Grading is usually on the bell curve, which means you are graded to each other.

How will you know if it's not working?

☐
　Low science GPA

☐
　Having to repeat several pre-requisites

☐
　A declining science GPA

☐
　Lower-than-average DAT scores

You now have the opportunity to see what a real-life rejection letter looks like. I have included it for your reading pleasure.

Dear Mr. Tsuhako:

Your preliminary materials for admission to the University have been received and reviewed. From the information supplied, it does not appear that you are in a favorable position to be invited to an interview. Our decision is based on a comparison of your credentials with those of other non-resident applicants.

Last year over seven hundred non-residents made application for admission to our dental education program. Since the University is a state-supported institution, the College's entering first-year class is drawn mainly from the in-state applicant pool. Of approximately fifty students who enroll annually, usually only about fifteen students are from out-of-state. In order to save applicants and our own Admissions Committee time and expense, only those out-of-state applicants with the strongest grade point averages, Dental Admission Test scores and records of leadership and service are invited to complete the application process.

Your interest in our College is certainly appreciated. If we may be of assistance to you in the future, do not hesitate to contact us. We will be glad to help you in every way possible. Best wishes with your future plans!

Sincerely yours,

XXX XXXXX

Chairman, Admission Committee


So there you have it. You have seen what a rejection letter looks like. Now just be sure you don't get one! In reality there's a good chance you will. Most applicants don't get accepted by every school they apply to.

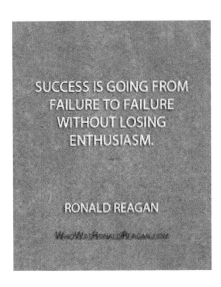

Possible reasons a person may not get in dental school:

- GPA/DAT was too low

- They want you to get a master's degree

- They want you to mature

- Too many barriers to achievement

- They are not sure of your commitment to dental school

- They are not sure if you can complete the program

- They are not sure you would make a good dentist

Maybe they want you to have more dental experience or a higher GPA; the list can go on and on. This is why you should contact the school.

## DENTAL SUPPORTING STAFF

Some supporting dental staff will attempt to advance their careers by applying to dental school. Hygienists, foreign students, dental technicians, and dental assistants will try to become a dentist. There are some pre-meds that decide to apply to dental school as their Plan B.

*Dentist* : typically four years of college with four years of dental school.

*Dental hygienist:* four-year degree. Cleans teeth and instructs patients how to take care of their teeth and gums.

*Dental assistant:* varies from community colleges to trade schools to dental schools.

*Dental technician:* two-year AA degree or trade school. Fabricates dentures, crowns and bridges. Some dental technicians own their own business, but this is an industry in transition.

*Support staff for the dental practice:* from office manager to bookkeeper.

Allied fields:

*Chiropractor:* can be an option for those who don't get into dental school.

*Optometrist:* equally as hard, but can be an option for some.

*Graduate school:* sometimes admissions will want you to enter a master's program before re-applying.

I have seen others go into law, MBA or CPA programs, even certification for teaching science in high school, a master's in science, a PhD, and associated dental positions such as hygienist, technician, assistant and cosmetologist.

# CHAPTER SEVEN

# Dental Laboratory

**SOME DENTAL SCHOOLS** offer pre-dental classes where you can learn dental laboratory procedures like setting denture teeth. Imagine starting dental school knowing how to pour impressions or how to set dentures. You can save yourself time now and save yourself stress later—once you start dental school you are going to be extremely busy.

## HOW TO POUR IMPRESSIONS

It's probably better to learn this before dental school. Pouring your first impression can be pretty stressful. I had gone from music school to dental lab school; the powder, vibrator and impression looked foreign to me. The loud buzzing of the vibrator sent tingles of panic up my back; the faint smell of the stone reminded me of the dentist's office. Pouring your first impression will be stressful, but in time it will be easy. The main thing is to avoid trapping air bubbles.

### See one, do one, teach one

**Step one:** first of all you need a clean and safe impression. Impressions should be sterilized to kill harmful bacteria and viruses. These chemicals be can sprayed or dipped. After 30 minutes or so, they can be rinsed off. Most likely you will pour a mold when you are pouring your first impression.

**Step two:** blow off the excess water with an air hose. A gentle gust of wind is all you need. The impression must be damp (no pooling of water or the stone will get chalky) something like the texture of jello, not completely dry, yet has some moisture to aid in the flow of stone.

**Step three:** in most cases you will be using yellow stone. The powder and water should be mixed to a thick consistency (a little thicker than pudding), but thin enough to flow within the cavities of the impressions. You'll want to fill one side and watch the stone flow in and out of the depressions, careful not to trap bubbles. The last step is to put a half-inch base of stone on the impression. Relax. As long as you are careful and follow good technique you will master these procedures. If tradespeople (dental assistants and technicians) routinely do it, it shouldn't be a problem for the dental student.

*Technician's tip:* in five minutes or so, the stone will start to set up and will become hard like cement.

## DENTAL STONES

**Plaster:** known for its white color and universal use from mounting models on articulators to investing dentures. The strength is similar to plaster of Paris. Soft.

153

*Yellow stone*: yellow in color and used to pour alginate impressions. Commonly referred to as model stone. Medium hardness.

*Die stone*: the hardest stone, used to make crown and bridge models where margin integrity is important. Die stone comes in a variety of colors such as blue, peach, white, pink, green, and light yellow. Hard.

*Technician's tip:* if you can't see the margin, apply water and the edge will stand out.

The vibrator aids in the flow of stone. There is a knob where you can adjust the strength and there is approximately five minutes of working time.

Well there you go—after 30 minutes it's ready to separate and trim.

*Technician's tip:* the longer you let the model set the harder it gets.

Materials for pouring impressions:

Mixing bowl, usually green or black rubber

Spatula

Vibrator

Stone (powder)

Lab knife

Model trimmer

Air hose attached to an air compressor

Debubbilizer spray acts as a surfactant (aids in flow) on rubber-based impressions

A mask, goggles, and sterilizing chemical (gloves) should be worn and proper ventilation is needed

*Technician's tip:* you will want to clean the bowl before it starts to harden. Once it sets (gets hard) it becomes a chore to clean.

Where can you get practice in pouring impressions?

A dental office

*Technician's tip:* generally the thicker you mix the stone, the harder it will get.

Model Trimmer

This is an example of a model trimmer. This type has a water source to keep the dust to a minimum. They are usually located near a sink (for the water source) and the on/off switch is located in the back.

You must be careful when using a model trimmer. You want to keep your fingers away from the cutting stone. It can be dangerous. This is best done by holding both sides of the model. First trim the back of the model to give you a flat, safe surface to work with. Then trim the back portion. From there you can trim around the model to give it a smooth professional look.

## CARVING A CROWN OUT OF PLASTER

*What is it?*

Basically it's carving a tooth (root included) out of yellow stone.

*Where can you find the sticks?*

You can find the sticks (they are poured up in a rubber mold) at dental schools. Some dental labs might have them available for training future dental technicians.

Tools of the trade:

Lab knife

Calipers

Bard parker

Tooth anatomy book

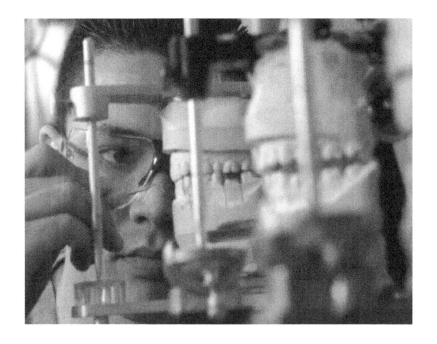

# WAXING A CROWN

Tooth waxing is something that you will see throughout your dental career. Waxing is the beginning step of learning tooth anatomy. Whether you carve in wax or stone the ability to carve a tooth is one of the building blocks of dentistry.

What it involves is heating up a waxing instrument, melting wax, adding the wax to a depression and carving a tooth out of the wax. The properties of wax are ideal in the making of crowns since it can be easily added and removed.

***Step one:*** planning and designing

*Step two:* carving to measurements

Tools of the trade:

#7 Waxer (this one is commonly used to melt wax)

Wax-carving instrument

Lab knife

Calipers

Alcohol lamp

Bunsen burner

# DRILLS IN THE DENTAL LAB

Drills have a variety of uses in the lab from grinding porcelain and finishing gold crowns to adjusting and finishing dentures.

*High-speed air-driven:* 350K rpm; in the lab, these are used to carve anatomy and finishing ceramic crowns. The high-speed drills are powered by compressed air supplied by a compressor. (Yes, the same ones that can be purchased at the home improvement stores. Usually the ones used in the dental office are quiet which means they are more expensive).

*High-torque systems:* 50K-40K-35K rpm, which means that they run smoothly and are good for general use and trimming margins.

**Belt-driven:** 20K rpm; the slow-speed drill is commonly known by its arm and belts that come in cloth or plastic. It is used as a general-use drill.

# ARTICULATORS

They are used to simulate the movements between the upper (maxillary) and lower (mandibular) jaw. Articulators come in a variety of styles:

- Adjustable

- Semi-adjustable

- Denture style with pin

- Crown & bridge with no pin: made in plastic and metal

- Disposable plastic articulators

# DENTURES

Some dental schools offer pre-dental classes where students learn to set-up a denture.

What you may learn:

Regular denture set-up

Mounting the case on an articulator

Fitting acrylic base plates

Making a bite block

Setting denture teeth

# PARTIAL DENTURES

A partial denture is like the word says: it's a *partial* denture. The thing that sets it apart from a complete denture is the partial denture framework. The framework is made in chrome and relies on clasps for retention. After the frames are cleaned and fitted to the model, denture teeth are set like a regular denture where it is then processed and finished.

# GOLD CROWNS

By the time you graduate dental school you will be an expert at full gold crowns or FGCs for short. You, the dental student, will fabricate a full gold crown as part of your training. Fixed restorations include gold and porcelain crowns, or any restorations that are cemented to teeth.

Gold crowns are prescribed when there's a substantial amount of tooth loss beyond the usual mercury filling. The crown is reduced for a crown (prepped) and an impression taken. The impression is poured, the model trimmed (and usually pinned), then mounted on an articulator, and the margins marked. A die spacer is painted to simulate cement and the crown is waxed, invested, cast, cleaned, finished and polished; then it is ready for cementation.

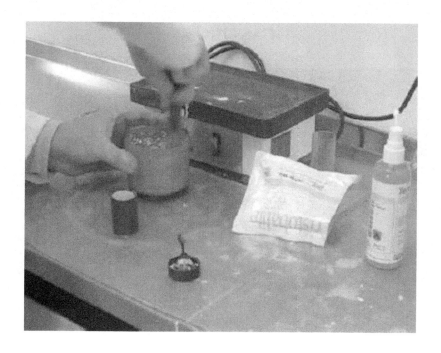

Investing

*Technician's tip:* this is how a gold crown is invested in a metal ring. After it sets it goes into the burnout oven.

# WAXES

There's a lot of wax in the lab. Just about every procedure involves some type of wax. There's crown and bridge inlay wax, margin wax, dipping wax, carving wax, diagnostic wax, sculpturing wax, and wax for anatomy. The waxes for dentures include baseplate wax, hard, medium and soft pink wax, and sticky wax for all-around purposes.

# CASTING

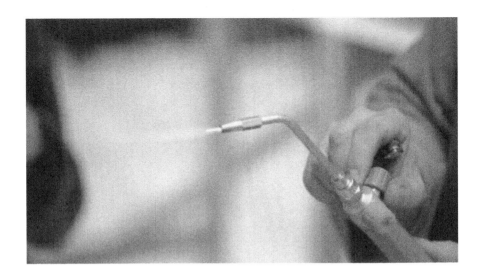

A soldering torch

This is my least favorite thing to do in the lab. It can be a scary thing to be standing there . . . a smoldering blue flame, hissing in your hand, while you are standing next to explosive gas and oxygen tanks a few feet away. You can take comfort from my experience—I never blew myself up, although I could have burned myself pretty bad.

In this lab procedure you are going to melt metal with a torch and the molten metal is going to shoot into an empty mold. This is the stage after the gold crown has been invested and is in the burnout oven. It was wax, but it has turned into a vapor and is gone. All that remains is an empty mold. This is known as the lost wax technique.

To set up the casting machine, wind the casting arm the indicated amount of turns, and use the pin to hold the casting machine arm in place. The more spins, the faster it goes and it operates on centrifugal force.

Light the torch starting with the gas first, then oxygen. The flame can be adjusted to the right temperature with the knobs.

The various metals act differently when they are melted. You have non-precious metal that slumps at a high temperature. Precious metal and gold spins when you look at the liquid metal. Semi-precious metal acts differently depending on the percent composition of precious metal.

Once the metal has been melted, open the oven and place the ring in the crucible (holder), reheat the metal and release the pin and then the arm. The casting machine will spin rapidly and centrifugal force shoots the metal into the space where the wax once existed. Never touch the ring as it is very hot. Allow to cool to room temperature. Turn off the torch and thank your God that you are still alive.

*Technician's tip:* always check the sprue hole and face the opening to you. Once I placed the flat area facing me and the melted metal hit the flat surface and sprayed liquid metal everywhere. By the time it hit my smock it had cooled off. Smoke rose up and it looked like I had been shot with a shotgun. No burns, no problem, just a ruined lab coat.

*Technician's tip:* when closing the torch, turn off the oxygen first and then the gas, or you will hear a loud pop!

# METAL

The percentage of gold in an alloy can be crucial for how well a crown will perform. Asking a lab technician, a sales rep or a metal manufacturer can help you to choose what type of metals to use. Don't be afraid to ask them. Generally the more gold, the softer the metal.

There's white gold, yellow gold, rose gold, high percent of gold, low percent of gold, precious, semi-precious and non-precious. If you like gold you have found the right calling. Dentistry has a lot of uses for gold. One great thing is that this colorful gold can be used to make jewelry as well.

Softer: a high percentage of pure gold can be extremely soft.

Hard: semi-precious metals are harder than precious.

Hardest: some metals can be extremely dense and hard. Non-precious is a dense metal.

# SOLDERING

Occasionally a gold crown will need a contact added or a hole to be filled. This is done by soldering. The first thing is to find solder that has a lower melting point than your gold crown. You want the crown to get hot, but not to melt before the solder. This takes practice and there is an art to soldering.

There are generally two ways to solder. One involves investing the crown, the other is directly heating the crown on a Bunsen burner.

163

The torch tip is different when soldering compared to casting. There is less gas and oxygen pressure and the addition of flux is important to help the solder to melt. A regular pencil lead can be used as a barrier (anti-flux) to stop the flow of metal.

# BURNISHING

There are times when you can "stretch" a margin, but dental school is not the time to be risking a margin that may flake away. Burnishing metal is a process where pressure is applied while slowly grinding metal that will stretch it. It can be an important technique to close an open margin.

Crown and bridge equipment and supplies:

Model equipment: vibrator, model trimmer, pins, saw, die spacer, die hardener, and die trimming burs.
Waxing: waxes, Bunsen burner, alcohol torch.
Investing: vacuum mixer, investment powder, rings, ring liners, debubblizers.
Casting: burnout oven, oxygen/propane or gas torch.
Finishing: burs, finishing discs.
Polishing: rubber wheels, brushes.

# CERAMICS

The history of the dental lab profession began as workers who were trained by dentists to do their tedious and time-consuming tasks for them. These procedures included gold crowns, dentures and ceramics. In time, lab technicians opened their own dental laboratories. When it comes to dental technology no other subject has received more attention than ceramics.

## How porcelain crowns are made

Let's assume the metal work has been completed for a PFM or commonly known as porcelain-fused-to-metal crown. The metal work is sandblasted and washed in an ultrasonic cleaner. A slurry layer of opaque (a wash coat) is applied and baked. After cooling, a second thicker layer is applied and baked. Opaque masks out the metal's grey color.

The porcelain body powder is mixed with buildup liquid or water and is built into a crown. Porcelain shrinks approximately 30% at this stage so the crown is overbuilt to accommodate for the shrinkage, then it goes into the porcelain oven for the first bake.

After the crown cools, it can be cut back to make room for incisal powders. These powders can include blue porcelain, translucent and incisal. Then it goes into the oven to be baked—this is commonly known as the second bake.

After cooling down, it will start to resemble a crown. We add a little translucent porcelain to fill in spaces where it is needed. From there it goes in the oven for the third bake.

*Technician's tip:* these bake cycles are programmed into the porcelain oven according to porcelain manufactures' instructions.

At this point the crown can be cut, ground and finished into the completed crown. The last step is stain and glazing.

The glaze powder is mixed with glaze liquid and applied evenly on the crown. If stain needs to be applied it is done at this step. Small corrections can be fixed with correction powder.

The last step is to polish the crown. And that's how a porcelain crown is made.

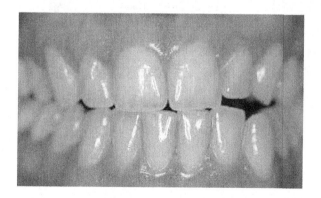

**Terms:**

**High-fusing porcelains** - are large-grained porcelains that are not as technique-sensitive.

**Fine-grained** is a higher-quality dental ceramic powder.

**Composite** - is a plastic material that is bonded via a blue light.

**Zirconia** is an all-ceramic material that can be milled and is commonly used with the CAD/CAM.

**PFM** or porcelain-fused-to-metal crowns.

Common metals that are used for porcelain framework:

- Non-precious

- Semi-precious

- Precious

# ALL-CERAMIC PORCELAINS

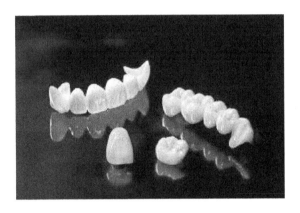

Zirconia restorations

These are restorations that are made up entirely of porcelain with no metal framework:

- Zirconia is a strong material that can be used for posteriors and anteriors.

- Alumina is not as strong and best for use on anterior crowns.

- Pressable crowns are waxed and invested.

- Veneers are thin layers of porcelain placed on the front of (the) anterior teeth.

166

*Technician's tip:* porcelain margins are PFMs (porcelain-to-metal crowns) with margins made in porcelain.

FOR THOSE DENTISTS WHO WILL HAVE THEIR OWN "IN-HOUSE" LABS

For dentists who want to bring their lab work "in-house" it will require approximately $5,000-$10,000 to bootstrap a basic dental lab. The highest costs are the porcelain oven and porcelain powders. A new oven costs around $2,000 and a set of porcelain powders costs $1,000-$2,000 depending on the brand. For dentists who want to stain and glaze their crowns there are portable stain and glaze furnaces.

Ceramic lab equipment and supplies:

Porcelain oven
Porcelain powder kits, including stain and glaze
Buildup instruments and brushes
High-speed handpiece
Low-speed handpiece
Sandblaster
Compressor
Discs, burs, grinding wheels
Polishing wheels
Casting wheel (same as gold work)
Burnout oven
Investing supplies: vacuum mixer
Model trimmer and supplies (same as gold)
Model-making equipment and supplies
Vibrator

# DENTAL LAB INDUSTRY

Finding the right dental labs to work with can help save you time and offer your patients the best products and services. Your best dental lab solution is probably a collection of labs:

- Denture lab
- Production crown and bridge
- High-quality ceramics
- Full-service commercial lab

The dental lab industry is being transformed by technology. The systems are making models, wax-ups, ceramic crowns, and even dentures. Smaller labs are closing and large corporate dental companies are coming in. Dentists are utilizing chairside milling machines that can fabricate a crown in less than two hours, offering their patients a one-visit crown.

## Interview with a Dental Lab Owner

*What is the hardest part of your job?*

Communicating with someone who is a doctor at my job.

*What is the best part of your work?*

Seeing patients who are happy with their crowns.

*What is the worst part about lab work?*

When dentists get upset.

*What is your biggest fear?*

That the CAD/CAM will replace all of the lab work.

*What is the biggest cause of remakes?*

Unclear communications, open margins and bridges rocking.

*What, if anything, can be done to reduce remakes?*

Metal and ceramic try-ins, custom shades, and diagrams on how a dentist wants a "special" crown would help.

*What is the most enjoyable part of your job?*

Staining and glazing.

*If you could change one thing about your job, what would it be?*

Being able to see satisfied patients. Seeing doctors that are pleased with restorations. We hear more bad than good.

*What advice, if any, could you give a new dentist in finding a lab?*

Try out several labs.

Interested in what dental lab technicians are reading? These magazines are free and have wonderful articles on the latest in dental technology. Some of the articles may interest the future dentist.

Dental Lab Products

IDT Inside Dental Technology

LMT Lab Management Today

Spectrum Dialogue

Want to see a porcelain build-up? There are demo lab videos on YouTube.

*Technician's tip:* a little recognition goes a long way with dental techs.

# MBA

**WITH RECENT** trends moving towards group practices and corporate dentistry, some dentists have been earning an MBA to go along with their dental degrees.

*What is it?* It's a dual degree with classes on marketing, finance, accounting, management, technology, economics, and human relations, among others.

How an MBA helps:

- Credibility
- Financial management
- Technology
- Marketing
- Strategy
- Networking opportunities
- Entrepreneurship

*How will you learn?* In this program a lot of the learning happens with your classmates in group projects.

# Conclusion

**WHILE MY DREAM** of becoming a dentist didn't materialize for me, I am cheering for you. It's my hope that you learned something from my mistakes. While I was taking the classes, I was busy and didn't enjoy learning the material. Looking back like this made me appreciate the effort and journey that I had taken over two decades ago. What struck me was how little things have changed. The DAT content is remarkably the same, with the exception of the computerized test and the testing centers.

You may have wondered if there was life for me after not getting into dental school. I recovered and went back to school to complete an MBA/BS where I eventually owned a dental laboratory for ten years. While my pre-dental education was an emotional roller coaster you will be interested in knowing that I had difficulty finding a comparable goal with the same high risk and rewards. I do have regrets that I didn't make it. My final thought to you is to give it your best. Those A's in your classes can payoff in the end.

I wish you the very best on your road to dental school and hope that your hard work will be met with open doors.

The End

**MY GRANDMOTHER WAS** the oldest daughter of a farmer; she wanted to become a kimono maker or a singer. Her father said, "A farmer is a farmer," and wanted her to marry her cousin. At the end of her life she was singing for her retirement home and had made her living as a seamstress. She finally found her happiness. My wish for you is that you find what makes you happy. That can be our greatest legacy . . . that we lived our best life.

**Resources:**

http://www.Ada.org: American Dental Association. For the list of schools and DAT information.

http://www.Adea.org: the voice of dental education. Publishes the Official Guide to Dental Schools.

http://www.Asdanet.org: a source of all things pre-dental, DAT and the application process.

http://www.Studentdoctornetwork: a great forum for all pre-dental students.

# References:

Books:

*Medical School* by Keith Ablow

*Getting Into Medical School* by Sanford Brown

*Preparing for the DAT* by Betz Publishing

*GAAPS*

*Kaplan*

*MCAT Research and Education Association*

*A Concise Dictionary of Biology* (Oxford reference)

Text books:

*Biology* Wessells and Hopson

*General Chemistry* McQuarrie and Rock

*Report: Socio-Economic Disadvantage and Experience in Higher Education* by Forsyth and Furlong.

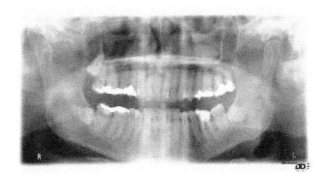

# DENTAL LAB GLOSSARY

**A**

**Accelerator** - something that is used to speed up setting time.

**Alcote** - a dental separator used in dentures.

**All-ceramic** – crowns that do not include metal.

**Anteriors** - are the front six teeth: centrals, laterals, cuspids.

**Articulating paper** - special paper that is used to mark occlusal contacts.

**Articulators** - are used to simulate the movements of the jaws.

**Atrophy** - the wasting away of tissue.

**Axis** - a straight line around things that rotate.

**B**

**Bite blocks** - are used as a guide to setting denture teeth.

**Block-out wax** - is used to fill in unwanted voids during die trimming.

**Bruxism** - is the grinding of the teeth.

**Buccal** - is the area facing the cheek and opposite the lingual/tongue.

**Burnout oven** - the investment ring is put in here to vaporize the wax in preparation for casting.

172

**CAD/CAM** - is a milled process where computer robotics makes crowns through computer-aided design and manufacturing.

**Ceramics** - from large-grained to fine-grained and the majority of crowns are made in some type of ceramic materials.

**Ceramist** - a dental technician who specializes in ceramics.

**Characterized denture** - is a high-quality denture that simulates gum and is sealed.

**Cingulum** - the bump on the lingual of anterior teeth.

**Composite** - is a plastic-like material that is cured with a blue light.

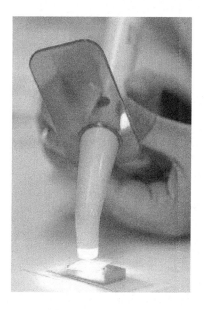

**Contact points** - the area where two teeth touch.

**Chrome** - removable partial dentures are sometimes made of this material.

**Cold cure acrylic** - a fast setting acrylic.

**Coping** - the metal work for a single-unit porcelain crown.

**Crucible** - the holding area where metal is melted during casting.

**Curve of Spee** - a relationship of dental curvature, from posterior to anterior/back to front.

**Curve of Wilson** - a relationship of side-to-side dental curvature.

**Cusp** - an elevation of the tooth on the occlusal surface.

**Cuspids** - are the sharp anterior teeth.

**Custom shade** - where the patient goes to the lab for shade matching.

**D**

**Debubblizer** - a spray that helps the flow of stone while pouring impressions.

**Decalcification** - white spots on teeth.

**Deciduous** - baby teeth.

**Dentin** - the body or the bulk of the tooth.

**Denture ID** - where the patient's ID is put in the denture.

**Diastema** - a space between the centrals.

**Digital impressions** - are a new method of impression-taking that utilizes digital photography.

**Distal** - is the area farthest away from the mesial.

**E**

**Edentulous** - without teeth.

**Enamel** - the hardest tissue in the human body. The outer layer of the tooth.

**Esthetics** - the fusion of beauty, shape and form.

**F**

**FGC** - full gold crown.

**Fossa** - is a pit, where three surfaces meet.

**Facial** surface is the tooth surface facing the face or lips.

174

**Festooning** - is a process in dentures that simulates natural shape and form.

**Flash** - the extra layer of acrylic that results from denture processing.

**Flask** - a metal flask that is used to process dentures.

**Flux** - a material that is used to remove oxides from molten gold during the casting process.

# G

**Gauges** - are used for metal and wax to measure thickness. Also referred to as calipers.

**Gingival** - the gum area.

**Gold scrap** - is a collection of gold crowns, grindings and dust that are sent to be recycled.

**Gypsum** - the material that makes up dental stone.

# H

**Hamular notch** - this is the area in the back of the maxillary palette.

**Hydrocolloid** - a duplicating material used to reproduce partial dentures. It's commonly made out of seaweed.

# I

**Immediate dentures** (or temporary dentures) - are made at the time of tooth extraction.

**Implants** - dental restorations that are supported by implants in the jaw bone.

**Impression tray** - a commercial or a custom tray used during impression-taking.

**Incisal** - the outer third of the anterior teeth.

**Interproximal** - the area between teeth.

# J

**Jaw** - is made up of the mandible (lower) and the maxilla (upper).

# K

**Knife-edge margin** - a type of margin prep.

# L

**Labial** - the surface of the tooth facing the lips, like the buccal surface of posterior teeth.

**Lateral** - tooth between the central and the cuspid.

**Lathe** - is used for denture finishing and polishing.

**Lingual** is the surface near the tongue.

**Lingual bar** - commonly found in mandibular partial dentures.

**Lingual rest** is a stabilizing rest on a partial denture.

# M

**Mamelon** - one of three rounded protuberances on the incisal surface.

**Mandible** - the lower jaw.

**Margin** - the border or the outer boundary of the die.

**Mastication** - the act of chewing.

**Materials** - are important in dentistry from the choice of impression materials to crowns.

**Maxilla** - the upper jaw.

**Metals** - high noble metal (90% Au and Pt); Medium noble metal (less than 90% but greater than 70%); low noble metal (less than 70%) and base metal is 0%.

**Metal finisher** - a dental technician who finishes (grinds) metal.

**Mesial** - the area facing the midline.

**Midline** - is the area between the two centrals.

**Miscast** - a situation where the ring is improperly cast (usually the wax was too thin in the crown) or the metal was not properly heated. The result is an incomplete casting.

**Model sealer** is a liquid that is painted on models to seal and harden them.

**N**

**Night guards** protect teeth at night.

**Non-precious** metal doesn't contain precious metals. An economical choice on crown and bridges. This metal is extremely hard and melts at a high temperature.

**O**

**Occlude** - to make the upper and lower teeth contact.

**Occlusal plane** - the horizontal plane between the maxilla (upper) and mandible (lower).

**Occlusal surface** - is the area (biting surface) of the posterior teeth where occlusion takes place.

**Occlusion (in)** - where opposing teeth are touching

**Occlusion (out of)** - where opposing teeth are not touching.

**Opaque** - a layer of material that masks out metal before applying porcelain.

**Open bite** - there is no contact between the upper and lower teeth.

**P**

**Palate** - the upper surface of the mouth.

**Peter K. Thomas** - is best known as the inventor of the PKT waxing and carving instruments.

**PFM** - porcelain fused to metal.

**Pit** - a small pinpoint depression.

**Porcelain margins** - or porcelain butt margins are usually used in the anterior crowns where the margins are made in porcelain.

**Porous** - contains unwanted bubbles.

**Pontic** - the part of a bridge that lies over tissue.

**Posterior teeth** - are the two bicuspids and three molars.

**Post** - it can be used as an ideal surface for a prep; replaces the root.

**Proximal** - the mesial and distal surfaces next to other teeth.

# Q

**Quadrant** - a quarter of the oral cavity. The maxilla (upper) and mandible (lower) are split in two sections each, making a total of four quadrants.

# R

**Reline** - adding a new base to a denture when the denture becomes loose.

**Remake** - a situation where a prosthesis has to be remade.

**Removable partial dentures** - are like dentures, but have clasps to hold them in place. Patients usually have some of their natural teeth left.

**Repair** - usually a repair of a cracked denture or a tooth that comes loose.

**Reservoir** - these little tags can help you when you do your gold crown casting to prevent pullback. A pullback or suck back can ruin a crown. The metal is pulled towards the opening of the ring.

**Ring liner** - is a form of cellulose that provides room for expansion during investing.

**Ringless investing** - a crown and bridge system that doesn't include a metal ring. It uses a silicon ring that is popped out before being put in the burnout oven.

# S

**Sandblaster machine** - cleans or prepares a surface by use of small particles and compressed air. Used to clean the inside of the crown before polishing and to prepare the surface of metal before applying opaque.

**Scales** - are used to weigh precious metals.

**Scrape** - one way to ensure that your contacts (the part where the teeth contact each other) is to scrape the adjacent teeth.

**Semi-adjustable articulators** - simulate jaw movements.

**Setting time** - the amount of time before a material starts to solidify.

**Sleep apnea** - devices are used to help reduce snoring.

**Soft-base** - dentures have a flexible tissue area.

**Sprue** - attaches the crown to the sprue-former during investing. It looks like a rope or spool of wax.

**Steamer** - cleans crowns with high-pressure steam.

**Surveyor** - an instrument that helps in planning the path of insertion and is used as an aid in planning implants, partial dentures and bridges.

**Sport guards** - used to protect teeth during contact sports.

**T**

**Temporal mandibular joint** (TMJ) - a joint between skull and mandible.

**Turnaround time** - the time it takes for the lab to make a restoration.

**U**

**Ultrasonic cleaner** - used to clean restorations after polishing.

**Undercut** - an area that is preventing the removal of an appliance or model. The path of insertion is one angle of relationship.

**Unilateral** - is a one-tooth partial denture.

**V**

**Vacuum mixer** - helps to reduce the bubbles out of stone and investment with vacuum pressure.

**Vacuum pump** - attached to the porcelain oven to supply vacuum pressure to remove bubbles from porcelain.

**Vibrator** - used to help the flow of stone while pouring impressions.

**Veneers** - are thin layers of porcelain used to correct minor imperfections in anterior teeth.

**W**

**Waxer** - a crown and bridge dental technician who waxes crowns and porcelain frameworks.

**Wax-up** - the finished waxing of teeth or dentures.

**Working model** - the model that is being used to fabricate the prosthesis.

**Whitening trays** - are used to hold bleaching gel.

**X**

**X-rays** - are sometimes used to check the micro fit of crowns.

**Y**

**Z**

**Zirconia** - is an all-ceramic material that is used to mill crowns via the CAD/CAM.

**Zygomatic muscle** - is an oblong, flat, and cylindrical muscle that draws the angle of the mouth upward.

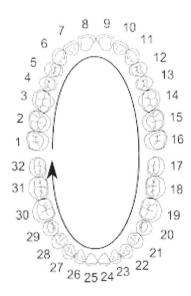

# THE TEETH

## Upper right quadrant

#1 wisdom tooth
#2 second molar
#3 first molar
#4 second bicuspid
#5 first bicuspid
#6 cuspid
#7 lateral
#8 central

## Upper left quadrant

#9 central
#10 lateral
#11 cuspid
#12 first bicuspid
#13 second bicuspid
#14 first molar
#15 second molar
#16 third molar

## Drops down to the lower left quadrant

#17 third molar
#18 second molar
#19 first molar
#20 second bicuspid
#21 first bicuspid
#22 cuspid
#23 lateral
#24 central

## Lower right quadrant

#25 central
#26 lateral
#27 cuspid
#28 first bicuspid
#29 second bicuspid
#30 first molar
#31 second molar
#32 third molar

**Biography:**

Cory M. Tsuhako, businessman, owner of Cory Tsuhako Enterprises, www.writingfordental.com and former owner of Coredent.com, an e-commerce and dental laboratory. He earned an MBA from National University; Bachelor of Science from California State University Dominguez Hills and is the author of three books. In his spare time he enjoys playing the guitar.

Other books:

*The Birth of a Business Life and Times of a Start up*

*Fatherlessness: America's Future?*

Made in the USA
Coppell, TX
27 July 2020